1st ed.

Country Weekend Knits

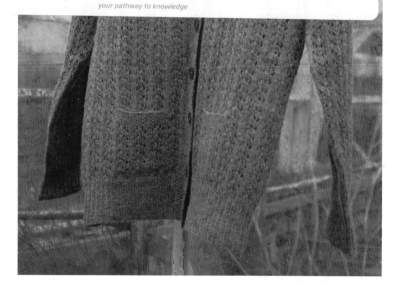

Country Weekend Knits

25 classic patterns for timeless knitwear

Madeline Weston

St. Martin's Griffin
New York

www.stmartins.com

Library of Congress Cataloging-in-Publication Data Available. Upon Request

ISBN-13: 978-0-312-38809-6
ISBN-10: 0-312-38809-8

First Edition: November 2008

10 9 8 7 6 5 4 3 2 1

Photographer's Assistant Heather Lewin
Studio Photographer Sian Irvine
Studio Photographer's Assistant Joe Giacomet
Stylist Stella Nicholaisen
Hair & Make up Sharon Ive

BMA Agency models Alla Sheptunova, Tralee Dunn, Alex Preston, Ali Zhanelova, Andy Young, Gemma Collingwood, Hannah Saunders

Locations
Knutchurch Estate
Ponttrilas, Hereford HR2 0DB
http://www.kentchurchcourrt.co.uk
Inglenook Camping Site
Hunstanton, Norfolk
trevor.arnold2@btinternet.com
Jeff Renant Farm
Wren Cottage, Kirk gate Street, Norfolk

Contents

Introduction

When I opened The Scottish Merchant in 1970 in London's Covent Garden, in partnership with my husband David Tomlinson, I had no idea that I would become fascinated by traditional knitting, or the slightest bit knowledgeable on the subject. The shop was originally a showcase for the best of Scottish crafts, including jewelry, glass, pottery, and textiles.

During the first year we were introduced to Margaret Stuart, who lived in Shetland. Margaret had a collection of old Fair Isle knitting, which had belonged to her grandmother and mother, and she was determined that the knitting heritage of the Shetland Islands should not disappear. She sent us a parcel of knitwear for our shop. I can still recall the excitement when we opened the first box, which contained pale, lacy shawls and scarves and vibrantly colored Fair Isle hats, scarves, and sweaters.

The Fair Isle knitwear that was available at this time was mainly in pastel colors; in particular, pullovers with round, star-patterned yokes were popular. The difference between these and the items Margaret sent us was enormous. We had never seen anything like her knitwear before; and neither had our customers, who were also amazed. By using the old patterns, with their strong bands, and the traditional colors originally obtained from vegetable dyes, Margaret's group of knitters were producing knitwear that was traditional yet stylish. Since Margaret was also a graduate of the Royal College of Art, her color sense was exceptional, and the shawls she sent us reflected the lovely heather colors of Shetland.

It was not long before we found that there were other gems of traditional knitting to be found in Scotland. We were approached by the parish priest of the remote isle of Eriskay, in the Outer Hebrides, asking if we would be an outlet for the local knitters there. These included only about a dozen knitters, and each of their ganseys, as they are called, took several weeks to knit. The sample that accompanied his letter was a masterpiece of patterning and construction. It was knitted in one piece, without seams, in a fine, tightly spun worsted wool, and was covered with textured stitch patterns with enchanting names, such as Marriage Lines and Tree of Life. The Eriskay gansey was immediately featured by Harpers & Queen magazine—then one of the world's ultimate style authorities.

At this time young knitwear designers began to work with color and pattern in a fresh way. Many of the now famous and established names were then exploring different approaches to knitting, and one journalist rightly called this the time of "the knitwear revolution."

This book sets out some of the old patterns from Scotland and other parts of the British Isles, along with designers' interpretations of them. The bold cables of Aran knitting and the subtle stitch patterns of ganseys are used here in a range of yarn weights, from fine mercerized cotton to robust Aran-weight yarn.

Preparing the book has brought back many happy memories of running the shop in Covent Garden and of long summer evenings in Shetland, and has spurred the renewal of old friendships. I am happy to introduce this book of classic and timeless patterns and hope you enjoy creating and wearing garments that have a direct link to the heritage of one of our oldest crafts.

Ganseys

The origins of the gansey, the traditional sweater worn by British fishermen, date back to Elizabethan times, when an enormous number of knitted garments were exported from the Channel Islands of Jersey and Guernsey. The word "gansey" may be derived from Guernsey, but there are marked differences between the Guernsey sweater and ganseys from other areas. The Guernsey is almost plain, and the sleeves are sewn in, whereas ganseys are often heavily patterned, and free of any seams.

The gansey is similar throughout Britain, in its seamless construction and its yarn, which is a hard 4- or 5-ply worsted, usually navy blue. However there are huge variations in pattern from one area to another; patterns were not written down but were passed to mother to daughter, and would be constantly altered and invented. The Scottish "lassies" who gutted the fish traveled south from Shetland during the herring fishing season, down the coast to Norfolk, providing the workforce needed there. Old photographs taken in the middle of the nineteenth century show fishermen wearing their ganseys, and the women knitting as they walked along the quayside at the end of their working day.

The distinctive features of the gansey arose from the need to produce a practical, hard-wearing garment that could be decorated with fancy stitches; because it was a working garment, it was given additional width beneath the armholes by the use of gussets. These allow ease of movement and prevent the garment from riding up. The cast-on for the ribbed waistband was often worked in a double thickness of yarn for additional strength.

The shoulder seams were joined by knitting the front and back together and binding off at the same time; this forms an attractive ridge at the top of the shoulder.

Sometimes this would be done inside the garment, with a "shoulder strap" of contrasting pattern knitted on one side of the join. The heavier stitch pattern that appears on the chest part of the gansey gives warmth where it is needed, but the sleeves were often totally or partially plain. These were worked by picking up the stitches at the sides of the armholes and knitting down toward the cuff, so they could be unraveled and reknitted when worn out. Old ganseys in various museums often show yarn of a completely different shade halfway down the sleeves where this repair has been made.

Because they were knitting in the round, the knitters always had the pattern facing them. In order to help calculate the position of the gusset and the stitch patterns, the knitter would often work two purl stitches in the stockinette stitch on either side of the body. Called "seam stitches" these often continue down the inside length of the sleeve.

The closeness of the knitting and the tightly spun worsted wool combine to make a wind-proof and nearly waterproof garment, which could be embellished with stitch patterns to satisfy the creative imagination of the knitter. Some of these represent things important to the everyday life of the fishing community: Anchor, Harbor Steps, Cable, Fish Net. Others are more emotive: Marriage Lines, Tree of Life, and Heart in Home.

The ganseys knitted by the wives for their menfolk were labors of love; the women could indulge their pride in their craft and produce an enormous variety of patterns from just knit and purl stitches. The men had their Sunday-best ganseys, which they would wear to church. In Cornwall a young bride would knit her future husband an elaborately patterned gansey called a "bridal shirt."

After the Industrial Revolution, when knitting frames largely replaced the hand-knitters, only the more remote areas continued to produce their hand-knitted garments. By the 1930s, the skills and patterns were fast disappearing; however, it would be only a little while before interested researchers would begin collecting patterns and old photographs to prevent this craft from dying out completely. The knitters of Eriskay, in the Outer Hebrides, are one of the last groups of women whose elaborately patterned ganseys still have the importance in the community that they did in many different fishing communities years ago.

Flamborough Fisherman's Gansey

This patterned gansey is knitted in the traditional way, in the round, so there's no sewing to be done at the end. It is based on a gansey belonging to one George Mainprize, who was born about 1875 in the village of Flamborough, on the Yorkshire coast.

Polperro Pattern Jacket

This warm Shetland wool jacket is beautifully patterned with chevron and seed stitch panels copied from a gansey worn in the picturesque fishing village of Polperro, Cornwall, around 1840. It has an easy and comfortable fit, and it can be buttoned to suit a woman or a man.

Newbiggin Pattern Sweater

Vertical panels of diamonds in knit and purl stitches decorate this generously sized sweater. The pattern originates in the fishing village of Newbiggin, on the Northumberland coast, and is here knitted in an Aran-weight, soft Shetland yarn.

Short-Sleeve Cotton Shirt

The texture of this stylish but simple shirt is provided by a variation of the Broken Diamonds pattern-a traditional gansey stitch. The crisp cotton yarn used here enhances the design, but another double-knitting-weight yarn may be used instead.

Jacob's Ladder Sweater

This pretty sweater features a saddle shoulder and traditional gansey stitches. There is a central panel of delicate cables and a Jacob's Ladder pattern, which is also repeated on the sleeves. Knitted in a lightweight cotton yarn, it could also be made in another yarn of the same weight.

Fife Banded Gansey

A simple version of an old classic—found as far afield as Scotland and Cornwall—this banded gansey has a yoke decorated with garter and seed stitches. The buttoned neck is typical of a Scottish gansey. Double knitting yarn makes a soft sweater, which also knits up quickly.

Sanquhar Gansey

The black and white knitting of Sanquhar, in Dumfriesshire, Scotland, has been incorporated in this warm sweater designed by a gansey knitter. This is called the Duke's Pattern and, like similar designs, was used to embellish the fine stockings and gloves for which the town was famous.

Eriskay Gansey

The Eriskay gansey is the most intricately patterned of all ganseys, originating from the tiny Gaelic-speaking island of Eriskay, south of South Uist, in the Western Isles of Scotland. Its patterns reflect the life of the fishermen: fishing nets, waves, anchor, horseshoe, cables, and starfish.

Caister Fisherman's Gansey

This traditional Norfolk gansey has a yoke patterned with seed stitch above a band of "rig and furrow"; this stitch is repeated on the shoulder straps. The cables are unusual in having garter stitch panels at each side, which makes them stand out in high relief.

Flamborough Fisherman's Gansey

❋ MATERIALS

Yarn

7 [8, 9, 10, 11] x 100g (3½oz) balls
Frangipani 5-ply Guernsey wool (100%
wool, approx 245 yards [225m], shade
Denim; also available in 500g [17½oz]
cones, approx 1,240 yards [1,130m])

Needles

1 circular needle size 2 (3mm), 32 inches
(80cm) long
1 set double-pointed needles size 2 (3mm)

Notions

2 stitch holders

Special abbreviation

m1 Pick up loop lying between sts and k tbl

❋ MEASUREMENTS

To fit chest 36 [38, 40, 42, 44] inches (91
[97, 102, 107, 112]cm)
Actual chest size 39¼ [41¼, 43, 44½, 46½]
inches (100 [105, 109, 113, 118]cm)
Length from back neck 24 [24¼, 25½, 26,
26¾] inches (61 [62, 65, 66, 68]cm)
Sleeve seam 18 [18½, 19¼, 19¾, 20½] inches
(46 [47, 49, 50, 52]cm)

Gauge

28 sts and 38 rows measure 4 inches
(10cm) over stockinette stitch on size 2
(3mm) needles (or size needed to obtain
given gauge)

BACK AND FRONT

This garment is knitted in one piece to the
armholes. Using circular needle cast on 264
[272, 288, 296, 312] sts. Work
in rounds as follows:

Round 1 (P1, k2, p1) to end.
Rep last round until rib measures 3 [3, 3½, 3½,
4] inches (8 [8, 9, 9, 10]cm).
Next round **P1, k13 [12, 11, 8, 9], *inc in
next st, k12 [10, 14, 12, 16]; rep from * 7 [9, 7,
9, 7] times, inc in next st, k12 [11, 10, 7, 8], p1;
rep from ** once more. *282 [294, 306, 318,
330] sts.*
Next round *P1, k139 [145, 151, 157, 163],
p1; rep from * once.
Rep last round 10 times. Begin patt.
Round 1 **P1, k13, *p8 [9, 10, 11, 12], k13; rep
from * 5 times more, p1; rep from ** once.
Round 2 **(P1, k6) twice, *p2, k4 [5, 6, 7, 8],
p2, k6, p1, k6; rep from * 5 times, p1; rep from
** once.
Round 3 **P1, k5, p1, k1, p1, k5, *p2, k4 (5, 6,
7, 8], p2, k5, p1, k1, p1, k5; rep from * 5 times,
p1; rep from ** once.
Round 4 **P1, k4, (p1, k1) twice, p1, k4, *p2,
k4 [5, 6, 7, 8], p2, k4, (p1, k1) twice, p1, k4; rep
from * 5 times, p1; rep from ** once.

Round 5 **P1, k3, (p1, k1) 3 times, p1, k3, *p2,
k4 [5, 6, 7, 8], p2, k3, (p1, k1) 3 times, p1, k3; rep
from * 5 times, p1; rep from ** once.
Round 6 **P1, k2, (p1, k1) 4 times, p1, k2, *p2,
k4 [5, 6, 7, 8], p2, k2, (p1, k1) 4 times, p1, k2; rep
from * 5 times, p1; rep from ** once.
Round 7 **(P1, k1) 7 times, *p2, k4 [5, 6, 7, 8],
p2, k1, (p1, k1) 6 times; rep from * 5 times, p1;
rep from ** once.
Round 8 As round 6.
Round 9 As round 5.

Round 10 As round 4.
Round 11 As round 3.
Round 12 As round 2.
These 12 rounds form patt. Cont in patt until
work measures 14¼, [14¼, 14½, 14½, 15]
inches (36 [36, 37, 37, 38]cm), ending with
round 12.

Shape for gusset

Next round *P1, patt 139 [145, 151, 157,
163], p1, m1; rep from * once.
Next round *P1, patt 139 [145, 151, 157,
163], p1, k1; rep from * once.
Next round *P1, patt 139 [145, 151, 157,
163], p1, m1, k1, m1; rep from * once.
Next round *P1, patt 139 [145, 151, 157,
163], p1, k3; rep from * once.
Cont in this way, inc 1 st at each end of each
gusset on next round and every foll alt round
until the round "*p1, patt 139 [145, 151, 157,
163], p1, k21; rep from * once" has been worked.
Work another 2 rounds.

Divide for front

Next round P1, m1, patt 139 [145, 151, 157,
163], m1 and turn; leave rem sts on needle.
Work backward and forward.
Next row (K1, p6) twice, *k2, p4 [5, 6, 7, 8],
k2, p6, k1, p6; rep from * 5 times, k1 and turn;
leave rem sts on needle.
***Cont in patt as follows:

Row 1 K6, p1, k1, p1, k5, *p2, k4 [5, 6, 7, 8], p2, k5, p1, k1, p1, k5; rep from * 5 times, k1.

Row 2 K1, p4, (k1, p1) twice, k1, p4, *k2, p4 [5, 6, 7, 8], k2, p4, (k1, p1) twice, k1, p4; rep from * 5 times, k1.

Row 3 K4, (p1, k1) 3 times, p1, k3, *p2, k4 [5, 6, 7, 8], p2, k3, (p1, k1) 3 times, p1, k3; rep from * 5 times, k1.

Row 4 K1, p2, (k1, p1) 4 times, k1, p2, *k2, p4 [5, 6, 7, 8], k2, p2, (k1, p1) 4 times, k1, p2; rep from * 5 times, k1.

Row 5 K2, (p1, k1) 6 times, *p2, k4 [5, 6, 7, 8], p2, k1, (p1, k1) 6 times; rep from * 5 times more, k1.

Row 6 As row 4.

Row 7 As row 3.

Row 8 As row 2.

Row 9 As row 1.

Row 10 (K1, p6) twice, *k2, p4 [5, 6, 7, 8], k2, p6, k1, p6; rep from * 5 times, k1.

Row 11 K14, *p8 [9, 10, 11, 12], k13; rep from * 5 times more, k1.

Row 12 As row 10.

These 12 rows form patt. Cont in patt until armholes measure 7½, [8, 8½, 9, 9½] inches (19 [20, 22, 23, 24]cm), ending with a wrong-side row. P 1 row***.

Shape neck

Next row P47 [49, 51, 53, 55] sts and turn; leave rem sts on needle.

Complete right front neck first.

Row 1 P1, (k1, p1) to end.

Rows 2–4 Purl.

Rep last 4 rows 4 times then rows 1 and 2 once. Leave these sts on spare needle. With wrong side of front facing, sl center 47 [49, 51, 53, 55] sts onto stitch holder, rejoin yarn to rem sts and p to end. Complete to match right front neck.

   With right side of back facing, sl first 23 sts onto safety pin, rejoin yarn, m1, patt 139 [145, 151, 157, 163], m1 and sl last 23 sts onto safety pin. Work backward and forward.

Next row (K1, p6) twice, *k2, p4 [5, 6, 7, 8], k2, p6, k1, p6; rep from * 5 times, k1.

Work as given for front from *** to ***.

Join shoulders

With right sides of back and front together, bind off 47 [49, 51, 53, 55] sts, taking 1 st from each needle and working them tog.

Sl next 47 [49, 51, 53, 55] center back sts onto stitch holder, rejoin yarn to rem sts and complete to match first shoulder.

NECKBAND

With right side facing and using double-pointed needles, pick up and k 17 sts down left front neck, k across 47 [49, 51, 53, 55] center front sts, pick up and k 17 sts up right front neck, k across 47 [49, 51, 53, 55] center back sts. *128 [132, 136, 140, 144] sts.*
Work 11 rounds in k2, p2, rib. Bind off in rib.

SLEEVES

With right side facing and using double-pointed needles, pick up and k 121 [127, 133, 139, 145] sts evenly around armhole edge, then p1, k21, p1 sts from safety pin. *144 [150, 156, 162, 168] sts.*
Work in rounds as follows:

Next round P to last 22 sts, k21, p1. Begin patt.

Round 1 K25 [26, 27, 28, 29], p2, k4 [5, 6, 7, 8], p2, *k6, p1, k6, p2, k4 [5, 6, 7, 8], p2; rep from * twice, k25 [26, 27, 28, 29], p1, yb, skpo, k17, k2 tog, p1.

Round 2 K25 [26, 27, 28, 29], p2, k4 [5, 6, 7, 8], p2, *k5, p1, k1, p1, k5, p2, k4 [5, 6, 7, 8], p2; rep from * twice, k25 [26, 27, 28, 29], p1, k19, p1.

Round 3 K25 [26, 27, 28, 29], p2, k4 [5, 6, 7, 8], p2, *k4, (p1, k1) twice, p1, k4, p2, k4 [5, 6, 7, 8], p2; rep from * twice, k25 [26, 27, 28, 29], p1, yb, skpo, k15, k2 tog, p1.

Round 4 K25 [26, 27, 28, 29], p2, k4 [5, 6, 7, 8], p2, *k3, (p1, k1) 3 times, p1, k3, p2, k4 [5, 6, 7, 8], p2; rep from * twice, k25 [26, 27, 28, 29], p1, k17, p1.

Round 5 K25 [26, 27, 28, 29], p2, k4 [5, 6, 7, 8], p2, *k2, (p1, k1) 4 times, p1, k2, p2, k4 [5, 6, 7, 8], p2; rep from * twice, k25 [26, 27, 28, 29], p1, yb, skpo, k13, k2 tog, p1.

Round 6 K25 [26, 27, 28, 29], p2, k4 [5, 6, 7, 8], p2, *k1, (p1, k1) 6 times, p2, k4 [5, 6, 7, 8], p2; rep from * twice, k25 [26, 27, 28, 29], p1, k15, p1.

Round 7 K25 [26, 27, 28, 29], p2, k4 [5, 6, 7, 8], p2, *k2, (p1, k1) 4 times, p1, k2, p2, k4 [5, 6, 7, 8], p2; rep from * twice, k25 [26, 27, 28, 29], p1, yb, skpo, k11, k2 tog, p1.

Round 8 K25 [26, 27, 28, 29], p2, k4 [5, 6, 7, 8], p2, *k3, (p1, k1) 3 times, p1, k3, p2, k4 [5, 6, 7, 8], p2; rep from * twice, k25 [26, 27, 28, 29], p1, k13, p1.

Round 9 K25 [26, 27, 28, 29], p2, k4 [5, 6, 7, 8], p2, *k4, (p1, k1) twice, p1, k4, p2, k4 [5, 6, 7, 8], p2; rep from * twice, k25 [26, 27, 28, 29], p1, yb, skpo, k9, k2 tog, p1.

Round 10 K25 [26, 27, 28, 29], p2, k4 [5, 6, 7, 8], p2, *k5, p1, k1, p1, k5, p2, k4 [5, 6, 7, 8], p2; rep from * twice, k25 [26, 27, 28, 29], p1, k11, p1.

Round 11 K25 [26, 27, 28, 29], p2, k4 [5, 6, 7, 8], p2, *k6, p1, k6, p2, k4 [5, 6, 7, 8], p2; rep from * twice, k25 [26, 27, 28, 29], p1, yb, skpo, k7, k2 tog, p1.

Round 12 K25 [26, 27, 28, 29], p8 [9, 10, 11, 12], *k13, p8 [9, 10, 11, 12]; rep from * twice, p1, k9, p1.

These 12 rounds establish patt. Cont in patt as set, dec 1 st at each end of gusset on next round and 2 foll alt rounds. Work 1 round straight.

Next round Patt 121 [127, 133, 139, 145], p1, yb, sl 1, k2 tog, psso, p1.

Next round Patt 121 [127, 133, 139, 145], p1, k1, p1.

Next round Patt 121 [127, 133, 139, 145], p2 tog, p1.

Next round Patt 121 [127, 133, 139, 145], p2. Repeat last round twice.

Next round Skpo, patt to last 4 sts, k2 tog, p2. Rep last 4 rounds 8 times. Work 3 rounds straight.

Next round Skpo, k to last 4 sts, k2 tog, p2.
Next 3 rounds K to last 2 sts, p2.
Rep last 4 rounds until 69 [73, 77, 85, 89] sts rem. Cont straight until sleeve measures 15 [15¼, 15¾, 16, 16½] inches (38 [39, 40, 41, 42]cm).

Next round K7, *k2 tog, k11 [12, 13, 15, 16]; rep from * to last 10 sts, k2 tog, k6 p2. *64 [68, 72, 80, 84] sts.*
Work 3¼ [3¼, 3½, 3½, 4] inches (8 [8, 9, 9, 10]cm) in rounds of k2, p2 rib. Bind off in rib.

FINISHING

Block as given on page 139 if you like.

Polperro Pattern Jacket

✻ MATERIALS

Yarn

22 x 50g (1¾oz) balls Jamieson's Shetland Heather Aran (100% pure Shetland wool, approx 101 yards [92m], shade 1390 Highland Mist

Note

The yarn is used double throughout

Needles

1 pair size 10½ (6.5mm)

1 pair size 11 (7.5mm)

Notions

8 buttons, 1¼ inches (3cm) in diameter

2 buttons, 1 inch (2.5cm) in diameter

✻ MEASUREMENTS

To fit chest 36–40 [42–46] inches (91–102 [107–116]cm)

Actual chest size 46 [52¼] inches (117 [133]cm)

Length to back neck 25½ [27] inches (65 [69]cm)

Sleeve seam 17¾ [19¼] inches (45 [49]cm)

Gauge

12 sts and 18 rows measure 4 inches (10 cm) over pattern on size 11 (7.5mm) needles (or size needed to obtain given gauge)

POCKET LININGS

Using larger needles and 2 strands of yarn together, cast on 13 [17] sts. Beg with a k row, work 12 rows in St st. Leave sts on a spare needle. Make another pocket lining to match.

RIGHT FRONT

Woman's jacket

Using smaller needles and 2 strands of yarn together, cast on 35 [41] sts.

Row 1 (Right side) K1, (p1, k1) to end.

Row 2 (P1, k1) to last 7 [9] sts, k1, (p1, k1) to end.

These 2 rows form seed st and rib patt.

Row 3 Patt 3 [4], bind off 1, patt to end.

Row 4 Patt to end, casting on 1 st over the 1 st bound off in previous row.

Rows 5–14 Rep rows 1 and 2, 5 times.

Row 15 As row 3.

Row 6 Patt 3, *inc in next st, patt 4 [5]; rep from * 3 times, inc in next st, patt 7 [8], cast on 1, patt to end. *40 [46] sts.*

Change to larger needles. Begin main patt.

Row 1 K1, (p1, k1) 3 [4] times, *(k5, p1) twice, (k1, p1) 2 [3] times; rep from * once, k1.

Row 2 K1, *(p1, k1) 2 [3] times, p5, k1, p1, k1, p4; rep from * once, k1, (p1, k1) 3 [4] times.

Row 3 K1, (p1, k1) 3 [4] times, *(k3, p1) 3 times, (k1, p1) 2 [3] times; rep from * once, k1.

Row 4 K1, *(p1, k1) 2 [3] times, p3, k1, p5, k1, p2; rep from * once, k1, (p1, k1) 3 [4] times.

Row 5 K1, (p1, k1) 3 [4] times, *k1, p1, k7, p1, (k1, p1) 3 [4] times; rep from * once, k1.

Row 6 K1, *(p1, k1) 3 [4] times, p9, k1; rep from * once, k1 (p1, k1) 3 [4] times.

These 6 rows form main patt. Patt 4 [10] rows.

Next row Patt 3 [4], bind off 1, patt to end.

Next row Patt to end, casting on 1 st over the 1 st bound off in previous row.

Patt 6 [0] rows.

Place pocket

Next row Patt 14 [16], sl next 13 [17] sts onto stitch holder, patt across 13 [17] sts of pocket lining, patt to end. Cont in patt making buttonholes as before on foll rows 10 and 11 [16 and 17] and 3 foll rows 17 and 18.

Shape neck

Next row Patt 7 [9] and sl these sts onto safety pin, patt to end.

Patt 1 row. Bind off 3 [4] sts at beg of next row. Dec 1 st at neck edge on next 2 rows then on 2 [3] foll alt rows. *26 [28] sts.*

Patt 9 [7] rows straight. Bind off.

Man's jacket

Work as given for right front of woman's jacket omitting buttonholes.

LEFT FRONT

Woman's jacket

**Using smaller needles and 2 strands of yarn together, cast on 35 [41] sts.

Row 1 (Right side) K1, (p1, k1) to end.

Cheveron and seed stitch pattern

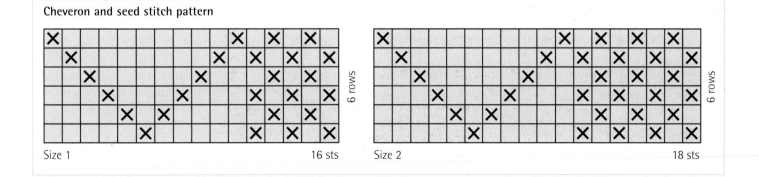

Size 1   16 sts   6 rows

Size 2   18 sts   6 rows

Row 2 K1, (p1, k1) 3 [4] times, (k1, p1) to end. These 2 rows form seed st and rib patt**. Patt 13 rows.

Next row Patt 11 [13], *inc in next st, patt 4 [5]; rep from * to last 4 sts, inc in next st, patt to end. *40 [46] sts.*

***Change to larger needles. Begin main patt.

Row 1 K1, *(p1, k1) 2 [3] times, (p1, k5) twice; rep from * once more, k1, (p1, k1) 3 [4] times.

Row 2 K1, (p1, k1) 3 [4] times, *p4, k1, p1, k1, p5, (k1, p1) 2 [3] times; rep from * once, k1.

Row 3 K1, *(p1, k1) 2 [3] times, (p1, k3) 3 times; rep from * once, k1, (p1, k1) 3 [4] times.

Row 4 K1, (p1, k1) 3 [4] times, *p2, k1, p5, k1, p3, (k1, p1) 2 [3] times; rep from * once, k1.

Row 5 K1, *(p1, k1) 3 [4] times, p1, k7, p1, k1; rep from * once, k1, (p1, k1) 3 [4] times.

Row 6 K1, (p1, k1) 3 [4] times, *k1, p9, (k1, p1) 3 [4] times; rep from * once, k1. These 6 rows form main patt***. Patt 12 rows.

Place pocket

Next row Patt 13, sl next 13 [17] sts onto stitch holder, patt across 13 [17] sts of pocket lining, patt to end. Patt 64 [70] rows.

Shape neck

Next row Patt 7 [9] and sl these sts onto safety pin, patt to end.

Patt 1 row. Bind off 3 [4] sts at beg of next row. Dec 1 st at neck edge on next 2 rows then on 2 [3] foll alt rows. *26 [28] sts.*

Patt 10 [8] rows straight. Bind off.

Man's jacket

Work as given for left front of woman's jacket from ** to **.

Row 3 Patt to last 4 [5] sts, bind off 1, patt to end.

Row 4 Patt to end, casting on 1 st over the 1 st bound off in previous row.

Rows 5–14 Rep rows 1 and 2, 5 times.

Row 15 As row 3.

Row 16 Patt 3 [4], cast on 1, patt 7 [8], *inc in next st, patt 4 [5]; rep from * 3 times, inc in next st, patt 3. *40 [46] sts.*

Work as given for left front of woman's jacket from *** to ***. Patt 4 [10] rows.

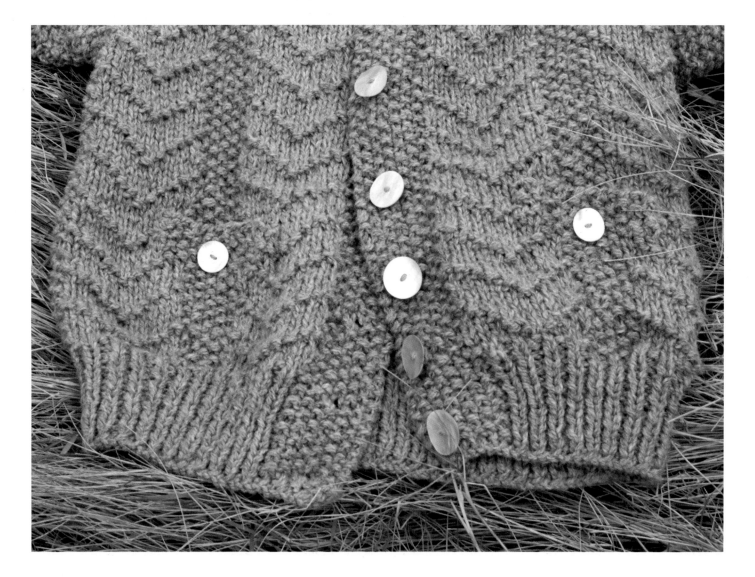

Next row Patt to last 4 sts, bind off 1, patt to end.

Next row Patt to end casting on 1 st over the 1 st bound off in previous row. Patt 6 [0] rows.

Place pocket

Next row Patt 13, sl next 13 [17] sts onto stitch holder, patt across 13 [17] sts of pocket lining, patt to end.

Cont in patt making buttonholes as before on foll rows 10 and 11 [16 and 17] and 2 foll rows 17 and 18. Patt 16 rows straight then work 1 buttonhole row.

Shape neck

Next row Patt 3 [4], cast on 1, patt 3 [4] and sl these 7 [9] sts onto safely pin, patt to end. Complete as given for left front of woman's jacket.

BACK

Using smaller needles and 2 strands of yarn together, cast on 60 [70] sts. Work 15 rows in k1, p1 rib.

Next row Rib 5 [4], *inc in next st, rib 4 [5]; rep from * to end. *71 [81] sts.* Change to larger needles. Begin main patt.

Row 1 (Right side) (K1, p1) 3 [4] times, *(k5, p1) twice, (k1, p1) 2 [3] times; rep from * to last st, k1.

Row 2 (K1, p1) 3 [4] times, *p4, k1, p1, k1, p5, (k1, p1) 2 [3] times; rep from * to last st, k1.

Row 3 (K1, p1) 3 [4] times, *(k3, p1) 3 times, (k1, p1) 2 [3] times; rep from * to last st, k1.

Row 4 (K1, p1) 3 [4] times, *p2, k1, p5, k1, p3, (k1, p1) 2 [3] times; rep from * to last st, k1.

Row 5 (K1, p1) 3 [4] times, *k1, p1, k7, (p1, k1) 3 [4] times, p1; rep from * to last st, k1.

Row 6 (K1, p1) 3 [4] times, *k1, p9, (k1, p1) 3 [4] times; rep from * to last st, k1.

These 6 rows form main patt. Rep these 6 rows 16 [17] times. Bind off.

SLEEVES

Using smaller needles and 2 strands together, cast on 32 [38] sts. Work 15 rows in k1, p1 rib.

Next row Rib 4 [3], *inc in next st, rib 3 [4]; rep from * to end. *39 [45] sts.*

Change to larger needles. Work 6 rows in patt as given for back. Cont in patt, inc 1 st at

each end of next row and every foll row until there are 63 [69] sts, working extra sts into St st. Work 3 [9] rows straight in patt.

Next row Inc in first st, (p1, k1) to last 2 sts, p1, inc in last st.

Next row P1, (k1, p1) to end.

Next row Inc in first st, (k1, p1) to last 2 sts, k1, inc in last st.

Next row K1, (p1, k1) to end.
Rep last 4 rows twice. *75 [81] sts.*
Bind off.

NECKBAND

Join shoulder seams. With right side facing, sl 7 [9] sts on right front safety pin onto smaller needle, using 2 strands of yarn together, pick up and k 18 sts up right front neck, 21 [23] sts across back neck, 18 sts down left front neck and k1, (p1, k1) 3 [4] times from left front safety pin. *71 [77] sts.*

Row 1 (Wrong side) K1, (p1, k1) 3 [4] times, k1, (p1, k1) to last 7 [9] sts, k1, (p1, k1) 3 [4] times.

Row 2 K1, (p1, k1) to end.
These 2 rows form seed st and rib patt.

Patt 1 row.

Next row Patt 3 [4], bind off 1, patt to end.

Next row Patt to end, casting on 1 st over the 1 st bound off in previous row.
Patt 2 rows. Bind off in patt.

POCKET EDGINGS

With right side facing and using larger needles and 2 strands of yarn together, rejoin yarn to the 13 [17] sts on holder, (k1, p1) 3 [4] times, bind off 1, p1 (st used in binding off), (k1, p1) 2 [3] times.

Next row (K1, p1) 3 [4] times, cast on 1, (p1, k1) 3 [4] times.

Next row K1, (p1, k1) to end.
Rep last row once. Bind off.

FINISHING

Block as given on page 139. Mark position of armholes 12 [13] inches (30 [33]cm) down from shoulders on back and fronts. Sew in sleeves. Join side and sleeve seams. Catch down pocket linings and sides of pocket edgings. Sew on buttons as shown, placing 2 smaller buttons at neck.

Newbiggin Pattern Sweater

Yarn

15 x 50g (1¾oz) balls Jamieson and Smith's Shetland Aran (100% pure new wool, approx 98 yards [90m]), shade SS11 (marine blue)

Needles

1 pair size 5 (3.75mm)

1 pair size 7 (4.5mm)

Special abbreviation

tw2 K into front of 2nd st then k first st, sl both sts off needle tog

❄ MEASUREMENTS

To fit chest 42–46 inches (107–117cm)

Actual chest size 49½ inches (126cm)

Length from back neck 26¾ inches (68cm)

Sleeve seam 19¾ inches (50cm)

Gauge

17 sts and 23 rows measure 4 inches (10cm) over patt on size 7 (4.5mm) needles (or size needed to obtain given gauge)

PATTERN PANEL

Repeat of 38 sts.

Row 1 (Right side) (P2, tw2) twice, k11, tw2, p2, tw2, p11, tw2.

Row 2 P2, k5, p1, k5, p2, k2, p7, k1, p5, (p2, k2) twice.

Row 3 (P2, tw2) twice, k4, p3, k4, tw2, p2, tw2, p4, k3, p4, tw2.

Row 4 P2, k3, p5, k3, p2, k2, p5, k5, p3, (p2, k2) twice.

Row 5 (P2, tw2) twice, k2, p7, k2, (tw2, p2) twice, k7, p2, tw2.

Row 6 P2, k1, p9, k1, p2, k2, p3, k9, p1, (p2, k2) twice.

Row 7 As row 5.

Row 8 As row 4.

Row 9 As row 3.

Row 10 As row 2.

Row 11 As row 1.

Row 12 P15, k2, p2, k11, (p2, k2) twice.

Row 13 (P2, tw2) twice, p5, k1, p5, tw2, p2, tw2, k5, p1, k5, tw2.

Row 14 P6, k3, p6, k2, p2, k4, p3, k4, (p2, k2) twice.

Row 15 (P2, tw2) twice, p3, k5, p3, tw2, p2, tw2, k3, p5, k3, tw2.

Row 16 P4, k7, p4, k2, p2, k2, p7, k2, (p2, k2) twice.

Row 17 (P2, tw2) twice, p1, k9, p1, tw2, p2, tw2, k1, p9, k1, tw2.

Row 18 As row 16.

Row 19 As row 15.

Row 20 As row 14.

Row 21 As row 13.

Row 22 As row 12.

These 22 rows form panel patt.

BACK

Using smaller needles, cast on 96 sts. Work 2¾ inches (7cm) in k1, p1 rib.

Next row Rib 9, (inc in next st, rib 5) to last 3 sts, rib 3. *110 sts.*

Change to larger needles. Begin patt.

Row 1 (Right side) (K2, p2) 3 times, tw2, rep row 1 of panel patt twice, (p2, tw2) twice, (p2, k2) 3 times.

Row 2 (P2, k2) 5 times, rep row 2 of panel patt twice, p2, (k2, p2) 3 times.

Row 3 (P2, k2) 3 times, tw2, rep row 3 of panel patt twice, (p2, tw2) twice, (k2, p2) 3 times.

Row 4 (K2, p2) 3 times, (p2, k2) twice, rep row 4 of panel patt twice, p2, (p2, k2) 3 times.

These 4 rows establish patt. Cont in patt as set, working appropriate rows of panel patt until work measures 25½ inches (65cm), ending with row 2 of panel patt.

Shape shoulders

Bind off 10 sts at beg of next 8 rows. Leave rem sts on spare needle.

FRONT

Work as given for back until front measures 24 inches (61cm) from beg, ending with row 14 of panel patt.

Shape neck

Next row Patt 49 and turn; leave rem sts on a spare needle. Complete left side of neck first. Dec 1 st at neck edge on next 9 rows.

Shape shoulder

Bind off 10 sts at beg of next row and 2 foll alt rows. Work 1 row. Bind off rem sts. With right side facing, sl center 12 sts onto a safety pin, rejoin yarn to rem sts, patt to end. Complete as given for left side neck.

Diamond pattern

22 rows

11 sts

SLEEVES

Using smaller needles, cast on 50 sts. Work
2¾ inches (7cm) in k1, p1 rib.
Next row Rib 2, (inc in next st, rib 3) to end.
62 sts.
Change to larger needles. Begin patt.
Row 1 (Right side) K9, tw2, p2, tw2, p11, tw2
(p2, tw2) twice, k11, tw2, p2, tw2, p9.
Row 2 K3, p1, k5, p2, k2, p7, k1, p5, (p2, k2)
twice, p2, k5, p1, k5, p2, k2, p7, k1, p3.
Row 3 K2, p3, k4, tw2, p2, tw2, p4, k3, p4,
tw2, (p2, tw2) twice, k4, p3, k4, tw2, p2, tw2,
p4, k3, p2.
Row 4 K1, p5, k3, p2, k2, p5, k5, p3, (p2, k2)
twice, p2, k3, p5, k3, p2, k2, p5, k5, p1.
These 4 rows establish patt. Cont in patt, inc
1 st at each end of next row and 4 foll row 5
then on every foll row 6 until there are 96 sts,
working extra sts into patt. Work 3 rows
straight. Bind off.

NECKBAND

Join right shoulder seam. With right side
facing and using smaller needles, pick up and
k 19 sts down left side neck, k across 12 center
front sts, pick up and k 19 sts up right side
neck, and k across 30 center back sts. *80 sts.*
Work 2½ inches (6cm) in k1, p1 rib. Bind off
in rib.

FINISHING

Block each piece as given on page 139.
Join left shoulder and neckband seam.
Fold neckband in half to wrong side and
slipstitch in place. Mark positions of armholes
10½ inches (27cm) down from shoulders
on back and front. Sew in sleeves between
markers. Join side and sleeve seams.

Short-Sleeve Cotton Shirt

❖ MATERIALS
Yarn
13 [13, 14] x 50g (1¾oz) balls Rowan handknit cotton (100% cotton, approx 93 yards [85m]), shade 251 Ecru
Needles
1 pair size 3 (3.25mm)
1 pair size 6 (4mm)
Notions
3 buttons, ⅝ inch (1.5cm) in diameter

❖ MEASUREMENTS
To fit chest 34 [36, 38] inches (86 [91, 97]cm)
Actual chest size 38 [39, 41] inches (96 [100, 104]cm)
Length from back neck 23¼ [24, 24½] inches (60 [61, 62]cm)
Sleeve seam 6 inches (15cm)
Gauge
20 sts and 32 rows measure 4 inches (10cm) over patt on size 6 (4mm) needles (or size needed to obtain given gauge)

BACK

Using smaller needles, cast on 98 [102, 106] sts. Work 1¼ inches (3cm) in k1, p1 rib. Change to larger needles. Begin patt.
Row 1 (Wrong side) P0 [2, 4], (p4, k6, p4) to last 0 [2, 4] sts, p0 [2, 4].
Row 2 Knit.
Rows 3 and 4 As rows 1 and 2.
Row 5 As row 1.
Row 6 K3 [5, 7], (p1, k6) to last 4 [6, 8] sts, p1, k3 [5, 7].
Row 7 P0 [0, 1], k0 [0, 1], p0, [2, 2], (p2, k1, p8, k1, p2) to last 0 [2, 4] sts, p0 [2, 2], k0 [0, 1], p0 [0, 1].
Row 8 K0, [0, 2], p0 [1, 1], k0 [1, 1], (k1, p1, k10, p1, k1) to last 0 [2, 4] sts, k0 [1, 1], p0 [1, 1], k0 [0, 2].
Row 9 p0 [1, 3], k0 [1, 1], (k1, p12, k1) to last 0 [2, 4] sts, k0 [1, 1], p0 [1, 3].

Row 10 As row 8.
Row 11 As row 7.
Row 12 As row 6.
These 12 rows form patt. Cont in patt until work measures 23½ [24, 24½] inches 60 [61, 62]cm, ending with a wrong-side row.
Shape shoulders
Bind off 34 [36, 38] sts at beg of next 2 rows. Bind off rem 30 sts.

FRONT

Work as given for back until work measures 15¼ [15¾, 16] inches (39 [40, 41]cm), ending with a right-side row.
Divide for neck opening.
Next row Patt 46 [48, 50], bind off 6, patt to end. Complete left side of front first. Cont straight until front measures 20½ [20¾, 21¼] inches (52 [53, 54]cm), ending at neck edge.

Shape neck
Bind off 6 sts at beg of next row. Dec 1 st at neck edge on every right-side row until 34 [36, 38] sts rem. Cont straight until front matches back to shoulder, ending at side edge. Bind off. With right side facing, rejoin yarn to rem sts and patt to end. Complete as given for first side of neck.

SLEEVES

Using smaller needles, cast on 70 [74, 78] sts. Work 1¼ inches (3cm) in k1, p1 rib. Change to larger needles. Cont in patt as given for back, inc 1 st at each end of 3rd row and every foll alt row until there are 98 [102, 106] sts, working extra sts into patt. Cont straight until work measures 6 inches (15cm) from beg, ending with a wrong-side row.
Bind off.

FRONT BANDS

Buttonhole band

With right side facing and using smaller needles, pick up and k 28 sts evenly along right side of neck opening. Work 3 rows in k1, p1 rib.

Buttonhole row

Rib 3, (bind off 2, rib 8 including st used in binding off) twice, bind off 2, rib to end.
Next row Rib to end, casting on 2 sts over those bound off in previous row.
Rib 2 rows. Bind off in rib.

Button band

Work as given for buttonhole band, picking up sts along left side of neck opening and omitting buttonholes.

COLLAR

Using smaller needles, cast on 103 sts.
Row 1 (Right side) K1, (p1, k1) to end.
Row 2 P1, (k1, p1) to end.
Rep these 2 rows until collar measures 2¾ inches (7cm), ending with a wrong-side row.

Bind off in rib.

FINISHING

Block each piece as given on page 139. Lap buttonhole band over button border and catch down at base of opening. Join shoulder seams. Sew on collar. Mark position of armholes 9½ [9¾, 10¼] inches (24 [25, 26]cm) down from shoulder on back and front. Sew in sleeves between markers. Join side and sleeve seams. Sew on buttons.

Jacob's Ladder Sweater

❉ MATERIALS

Yarn

9 [10, 11] x 50g (1¾oz) balls Rowan 4-ply cotton (100% cotton, approx 186 yards [170m]), shade 135 Fennel

Needles

1 pair size 1 (2.25mm)

1 pair size 3 (3.25mm)

1 cable needle

Special abbreviations

m1 Pick up loop lying between sts and work tbl

c6f Sl next 3 sts onto cable needle and leave at front of work, k3 from left-hand needle, k3 from cable needle

c6b Sl next 3 sts onto cable needle and leave at back of work, k3 from left-hand needle, k3 from cable needle

❉ MEASUREMENTS

To fit chest 34 [36, 38] inches (86 [91, 97]cm)

Actual chest size 36 [39½, 43½] inches (92 [100, 110]cm)

Length from back neck 21½ [22, 22½] inches (55 [56, 57]cm)

Sleeve seam 17¼ [17¾, 18] inches (44 [45, 46]cm)

Gauge

28 sts and 40 rows measure 4 inches (10cm) over stockinette stitch on size 3 (3.25mm) needles (or size needed to obtain given gauge)

BACK

Using smaller needles, cast on 109 [119, 127] sts.

Row 1 (Right side) K1, (p1, k1) to end.

Row 2 P1, (k1, p1) to end.

Rep these 2 rows until rib measures 4 inches (10cm), ending with row 1.

Next row Rib 10 [12, 10], (m1, rib 3) to last 6 [8, 6] sts, rib to end. *140 [152, 164] sts.*

Change to larger needles. Begin patt.

Row 1 K45 [51, 57], k1 tbl, p2, k6, p2, k1 tbl, k26, k1 tbl, p2, k6, p2, k1 tbl, k45 [51, 57].

Row 2 P46 [52, 58], k2, p6, k2, p28, k2, p6, k2, p46 [52, 58].

Row 3 K45 [51, 57], k1 tbl, p2, c6f, p2, k1 tbl, k26, k1 tbl, p2, c6b, p2, k1 tbl, k45 [51, 57].

Row 4 As row 2.

Rows 5–8 Rep rows 1 and 2 twice.

Row 9 As row 3.

Row 10 P46 [52, 58], k2, p6, k2, p1, k26, p1, k2, p6, k2, p46 [52, 58].

Row 11 As row 1.

Row 12 As row 10.

These 12 rows form patt. Cont in patt until work measures 13¾ [14, 14½] inches (35 [36, 37]cm), ending with a wrong-side row.

Shape armholes

Bind off 8 sts at beg of next 2 rows. Dec 1 st at each end of next row and every foll alt row until 102 [106, 110] sts rem. Cont straight until armholes measure 7 inches (18cm), ending with a wrong-side row.

Shape shoulders

Bind off 8 [8, 9] sts at beg of next 6 rows and 7 [9, 8] sts at beg of foll 2 rows. Leave rem 40 sts on a spare needle.

FRONT

Work as given for back until armholes measure 5 inches (13cm), ending with a wrong-side row.

Shape neck

Next row Patt 45 [47, 49] sts and turn; leave rem sts on a spare needle. Complete left side of neck first. Bind off 4 sts at beg of next row and foll alt row and 2 sts at beg of foll alt row. Dec 1 st at neck edge on foll 4 alt rows. *31 [33, 35] sts.* Cont straight until front matches back to shoulder, ending at armhole edge.

Shape shoulder

Bind off 8 [8, 9] sts at beg of next row and foll 2 alt rows. Work 1 row. Bind off rem 7 [9, 8] sts. With right side facing, sl center 12 sts onto a safety pin, rejoin yarn to rem sts and patt to end. Patt 1 row. Complete as given for first side of neck.

SLEEVES

Using smaller needles, cast on 60 sts. Work 3¼ inches (8cm) in k1, p1 rib.

Next row Rib 4, (m1, rib 4) to end. *74 sts.* Change to larger needles. Begin patt.

Rows 1–8 Beg with a k row, work 8 rows St st.

Rows 9–12 Knit.

These 12 rows form patt. Cont in patt, inc 1 st at each end of next row and every foll row 7 until there are 106 sts. Cont straight until sleeve measures 17¼ [17¾, 18] inches (44 [45, 46]cm), ending with a wrong-side row.

Shape top

Bind off 8 sts at beg of next 2 rows. Dec 1 st at each end of next row and every foll alt row until 28 sts rem. Work 4 [4¼, 4¾] (10 [11, 12]cm) straight on sts for saddle shoulder, ending with a wrong-side row. Leave sts on a spare needle.

NECKBAND

Join right sleeve saddle shoulder to back and front and left sleeve saddle shoulder to front. With right side facing and using smaller needles, k across 28 sts from left saddle shoulder, pick up and k 24 sts down left front neck, k across 12 center front sts, pick up and k 24 sts up right front neck, k across 28 sts from right saddle shoulder

and 40 center back sts. *156 sts.*
Work 7 rows in k1, p1 rib. Bind off in rib.

FINISHING

Block pieces as given on page 139. Join left saddle shoulder to back, then join neckband. Sew in sleeves. Join side and sleeve seams.

Fife Banded Gansey

❋ MATERIALS

Yarn

11 [12, 13, 14, 15] x 50g (1¾oz) balls
Jaeger Matchmaker merino double knitting
(100% wool, approx 131 yards [120m])
shade 789 Syrup

Needles

1 circular needle size 5 (3.75mm), 32 inches
(80cm) long; 1 set double-pointed needles
size 5 (3.75mm)

Notions

2 buttons, ⅝ inch (1.5cm) in diameter
2 stitch holders

Special abbreviation

m1 Pick up loop lying between sts
and k tbl

❋ MEASUREMENTS

To fit chest 36 [38, 40, 42, 44] inches
(91 [97, 102, 107, 112]cm)
Actual chest size 40 [42, 44, 45¾, 47¾] inches
(102 [107, 112, 116, 121]cm)
Length from back neck 23¼ [24¼, 25¼, 26¾,
27½] inches (59 [62, 64, 68, 70]cm)
Sleeve seam 18 [18½, 19, 19¼, 19¾] inches
(46 [47, 48, 49, 50]cm)

Gauge

26 sts and 34 rows measure 4 inches
(10cm) over stockinette stitch on size 5
(3.75mm) needles (or size needed to obtain
given gauge).

BACK AND FRONT

This garment is knitted in one piece up to the
armholes. Using circular needle, cast on 232
[240, 256, 264, 280] sts. Work in rounds as
follows:

Round 1 (K2, p2) to end of round.
Rep this round until rib measures 2¼ (2¼, 2¾,
2¾, 3¼) inches (6 [6, 7, 7, 8]cm).
Next round **K7 [5, 8, 5, 9], *m1, k10 [9, 11,
10, 12]; rep from * 9 [11, 9, 11, 9] times, m1, k7
[5, 8, 5, 9], p1, m1, p1**; rep from ** to ** once.
256 [268, 280, 292, 304] sts.
Cont in St st as follows:
Round 1 *K125 [131, 137, 143, 149], p3; rep
from * once.
Round 2 *K125 [131, 137, 143, 149], p1, k1,
p1; rep from * once.
Rep these 2 rounds until work measures
12¼ [12½, 13½, 14, 15] inches 31 [32, 34, 36,
38]cm, ending with round 2.
Change to yoke patt.
Round 1 Purl.
Round 2 *P126 [132, 138, 144, 150], k1, p1;
rep from * once.
Round 3 Purl.
Round 4 *K125 [131, 137, 143, 149], p1, k1,
p1; rep from * once.
Round 5 *K125 [131, 137, 143, 149], p3; rep
from * once.
Round 6 As round 4.
Rep rounds 1–3.
Shape for gusset
Round 1 *K125 [131, 137, 143, 149], p1, m1,
k1, m1, p1; rep from * once.
Round 2 *K125 [131, 137, 143, 149], p1, k3,
p1; rep from * once.
Round 3 *K1 [0, 1, 0, 1], (p3, k1) 31 [32, 34,
35, 37] times, p0 [3, 0, 3, 0], p1, k3, p1; rep
from * once.
Round 4 As round 2.
Round 5 *K125 [131, 137, 143, 149], p1, k1,
(m1, k1) twice, p1; rep from * once.
Round 6 *P2 [1, 2, 1, 2], k1, (p3, k1) 30 [32,
33, 35, 36] times, p3 [2, 3, 2, 3], k5, p1; rep
from * once.

Round 7 *K125 [131, 137, 143, 149], p1, k5, p1; rep from * once.

Round 8 As round 7.

Round 9 *K1 [0, 1, 0, 1], (p3, k1) 31 [32, 34, 35, 37] times, p0 [3, 0, 3, 0], p1, k1, m1, k3, m1, k1, p1; rep from * once.

Round 10 *K125 [131, 137, 143, 149], p1, k7, p1; rep from * once.

Round 11 As round 10.

Round 12 *P2 [1, 2, 1, 2], k1, (p3, k1) 30 [32, 33, 35, 36] times, p3 [2, 3, 2, 3], k7, p1; rep from * once.

Cont in this way, keeping cont of patt and inc 1 st inside border of 1 st at each end of each gusset on next round and 3 foll round 4. Work 1 round.

Next round *P126 [132, 138, 144, 150], k15, p1; rep from * once.

Rep last round once.

Next round *P126 [132, 138, 144, 150], k1, m1, k13, m1, p1; rep from * once.

Next round *K125 [131, 137, 143, 149], p1, k17, p1; rep from * once.

Rep last round twice.

Next round *P126 [132, 138, 144, 150], k1, m1, k15, m1, k1, p1; rep from * once.

Next round *P126 [132, 138, 144, 150], k19, p1; rep from * once.

Rep last round once.

Next round *K125 [131, 137, 143, 149], p1, k19, p1; rep from * once.

Next round *K125 [131, 137, 143, 149], p1, k1, m1, k17, m1, k1, p1; rep from * once.

Next round *P1, (k1, p1) 62 [65, 68, 71, 74] times, p1, k21, p1; rep from * once.

Next round *K125 [131, 137, 143, 149], p1, k21, p1; rep from * once.

Rep last round once.

Next round *K1 (p1, k1) 62 [65, 68, 71, 74] times , p1, k21, p1; rep from * once.

Next round *K125 [131, 137, 143, 149], p1, k21, p1; rep from * once.

Divide for back and front

Next row K125 [131, 137, 143, 149] sts and turn; leave rem sts on a spare needle.
Complete back first.
***Work backward and forward as follows:

Row 1 (Wrong side) K1, (p1, k1) to end.

Row 2 Knit.

Row 3 Purl.

Row 4 As row 1.

Row 5 Purl.

Row 6 Knit.

Rep these 6 rows 2 [3, 3, 4, 4] times.
K 1 row. P 1 row. K 2 rows. P 1 row. K 2 rows. P 1 row. K 1 row.

Row 1 Knit.

Row 2 Purl.

Row 3 K1 [0, 1, 0, 1], (p3, k1) to last 0 [3, 0, 3, 0] sts, p0 [3, 0, 3, 0].

Row 4 Purl.

Row 5 Knit.

Row 6 K2 [1, 2, 1, 2], (p1, k3) to last 3 [2, 3, 2, 3] sts, p1, k2 [1, 2, 1, 2].

Rep these 6 rows 3 times.
K 1 row. P 2 rows. K 1 row. P 1 row.

Shape neck

Next row P46 [48, 50, 52, 54], bind off 33 [35, 37, 39, 41], p to end.
Complete right shoulder first.

Next row K to last 2 sts, k2 tog.

Next row Purl.

Next row P to last 2 sts, p2 tog.

Next row Knit.

Next row P to last 2 sts, p2 tog.

Next row Purl.

Next row K to last 2 sts, k2 tog.
P 2 rows. K 1 row. P 2 rows. K 1 row.
Leave rem 42 [44, 46, 48, 50] sts on a stitch holder.*** With right side of back facing, rejoin yarn to rem sts, k2 tog, k to end.

Next row Purl.

Next row P2 tog, p to end.

Next row Knit.

Next row P2 tog, p to end.

Next row Purl.

Next row K2 tog, k to end.
P 2 rows. K 1 row. P 2 rows. K 1 row.
Leave rem 42 [44, 46, 48, 50] sts on a stitch holder.
With right side of front facing, sl 23 sts onto a safety pin, rejoin yarn to rem sts, k to last 23 sts and sl these sts onto a safety pin. Work as given for back from *** to *** but leave sts on needle.

Join shoulders

With back and front right sides together, bind off 42 [44, 46, 48, 50] sts taking 1 st from each needle and working into them tog. Work other shoulder in same way.

NECKBAND

With right side facing, using circular needle and beg 5 rows down from left back shoulder, pick up and k 4 sts to shoulder, 10 sts down left front neck, 33 [35, 37, 39, 41] sts from center front, 10 sts up right front neck, 10 sts down right back neck, 33 [35, 37, 39, 41] sts from center back and 6 sts up left back neck, then cast on 4 sts. *110 [114, 118, 122, 126] sts.*
Work backward and forward as follows:

Row 1 (Wrong side) K6, (p2, k2) to last 4 sts, k4.

Row 2 K4, (p2, k2) to last 6 sts, p2, k4.

Row 3 As row 1.

Row 4 K2, yo, k2 tog, rib to last 4 sts, k4.
Rep rows 1 and 2 twice, then work rows 3 and 4. Work 1 row. Bind off in rib. Lap the first 4 sts over the cast-on sts and catch down the cast-on sts to wrong side. Sew on buttons.

SLEEVES

With right side facing and using double-pointed needles, pick up and k 88 [96, 96, 104, 104] sts evenly around armhole then p1, k21, p1 from safety pin. Work in rounds as follows:

Next round P89 [97, 97, 105, 105], k21, p1.
Rep last round once.

Next round P89 [97, 97, 105, 105], skpo, k17, k2 tog, p1.
Begin patt.

Round 1 K88 [96, 96, 104, 104], p1, k19, p1.

Round 2 (P1, k1) to last 21 sts, p1, k19, p1.

Round 3 As round 1.

Round 4 (K1, p1) to last 21 sts, p1, skpo, k15, k2 tog, p1.
These 4 rounds establish patt.

Next round Patt 88 [96, 96, 104, 104], p1, k17, p1.
Rep last round twice.

Next round Patt 88 [96, 96, 104, 104], p1, skpo, k13, k2 tog, p1.

Next round Patt 88 [96, 96, 104, 104], p1, k15, p1.
Rep last round twice.

Cont in this way, keeping cont of patt and dec 1 st inside border of 1 st at each end of gusset on next round and 3 foll 4th rounds.
Work 3 rounds.

Next round P89 [97, 97, 105, 105], skpo, k3,

k2 tog, p1.
Next round P89 [97, 97, 105, 105], k5, p1.
Rep last round once.
Next round K88 [96, 96, 104, 104], p1, k5, p1.
Next round K88 [96, 96, 104, 104], p1, skpo, k1, k2 tog, p1.
Next round K88 [96, 96, 104, 104], p1, k3, p1.
Next round P89 [97, 97, 105, 105], k3, p1.
Rep last round once.
Next round P89 [97, 97, 105, 105], sl 1, k2 tog, psso, p1.

Cont in St st as follows:
Next round K88 [96, 96, 104, 104], p3.
Next round K88 [96, 96, 104, 104], p1, k1, p1.
Work 2 rounds.
Next round Skpo, k84 [92, 92, 100, 100], k2 tog, p3.
Cont in this way, dec 1 st at beg and end of St st part on every foll round 11 [9, 10, 7, 8] round until 73 [75, 77, 79, 81] sts rem.
Cont straight until sleeve measures 15¾ [16, 16, 16, 16½] inches (40 [41, 41, 41, 42]cm).

Next round K6 [5, 5, 7, 7], *k2 tog, k6 [10, 7, 10, 7]; rep from * 6 [4, 6, 4, 6] times, k2 tog, k6 [5, 4, 7, 6], p2 tog, p1.
64 [68, 68, 72, 72] sts.
Work 2¼ [2¼, 2¾, 3¼, 3¼] inches (6 [6, 7, 8, 8]cm) in rounds of k2, p2 rib.
Bind off in rib.

FINISHING

Block as given on page 139.

Sanquhar Gansey

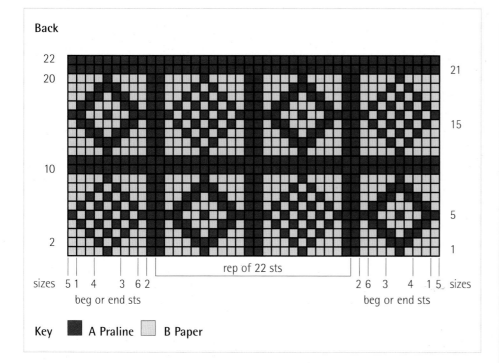

Back

22
20
21
15
10
5
2
1

rep of 22 sts

sizes 5 1 4   3 6 2   2 6 3   4   1 5 sizes
beg or end sts   beg or end sts

Key ■ A Praline ☐ B Paper

❈ MATERIALS

Yarn
Rowan Pure Wool Aran (approx 186 yards [170m])
A: 5 [5, 6, 6, 7, 7] x 100g (3½oz) balls, shade 677 Praline
B: 4 [5, 5, 6, 6, 7] x 100g (3½oz) balls, shade 671 Paper

Needles
1 pair size 6 (4mm)
1 pair size 7 (4.5mm)
1 set double-pointed needles size 7 (4.5mm)

Notions
2 stitch holders

❈ MEASUREMENTS

To fit chest 34 [36, 38, 40, 42, 44] inches (86 [91, 97, 102, 107, 112]cm)
Actual chest size 41, 43¼, 45¾, 48, 50½, 52¾ inches
(104 [110, 116, 122, 128, 134]cm)
Length from back neck 24½ [24½, 24½, 26, 26, 26] inches (62 [62, 62, 66, 66, 66]cm)
Sleeve seam 17½ [17½, 18, 19¼, 19¼, 19¾] inches
(45 [45, 46, 49, 49, 50]cm)

Gauge
20 sts and 22 rows measure 4 inches (10cm) over pattern on size 7 (4.5mm) needles (or size needed to obtain given gauge

BACK

Using smaller needles and yarn A, cast on 96 [100, 108, 112, 120, 124] sts.
Carry yarn not in use loosely across wrong side of work. Cont as follows:
Row 1 (Right side) (K2B, p2A) to end.
Row 2 (K2A, p2B) to end.
Rep these 2 rows until rib measures 2¼ inches (6cm), ending with row 2. Change to larger needles.
Next row Using yarn A, k7 [6, 9, 6, 6, 7], *inc in next st, k8 [7, 9, 8, 11, 9]; rep from * to last 8 [6, 9, 7, 6, 7] sts, inc in next st, k to end. *106 [112, 118, 124, 130, 136] sts.*
P1 row in yarn A. Beg with a k row, cont in St st and patt from chart for back, working odd-numbered (k) rows from right to left and even-numbered (p) rows from left to right until work measures approx 24½ [24½, 24½, 26, 26, 26] inches (62 [62, 62, 66, 66, 66]cm), ending with row 10 [10, 10, 22, 22, 22]. Leave these sts on a spare needle.

FRONT

Work as given for back, until front measures 12 rows less than back.
Shape neck
Next row Patt 44 [46, 48, 50, 52, 54] sts and turn; leave rem sts on a spare needle.
Complete left side of neck first. Bind off 3 sts at beg of next row and foll alt row and 2 sts at beg of foll 2 alt rows. Patt 4 rows straight. *34 [36, 38, 40, 42, 44] sts.*
Join left shoulder
With back and front wrong sides together and using yarn A, bind off 34 [36, 38, 40, 42, 44] sts taking 1 st from each needle and working them tog. Sl next 38 [40, 42, 44, 46, 48] sts on back onto a stitch holder. With right side of front facing, sl center 18 [20, 22, 24, 26, 28] sts onto a stitch holder, rejoin yarns to rem sts and patt to end. Patt 1 row. Bind off 3 sts at beg of next row and foll alt row and 2 sts at beg of foll 2 alt rows. Patt 3 rows straight. *34 [36, 38, 40, 42, 44] sts.*

Join right shoulder
Work as given for left shoulder.

SLEEVES

Using smaller needles and yarn A, cast on 44 [44, 48, 48, 52, 52] sts. Work 2¼ inches (6cm) in rib as given for back waistband, ending with row 2. Change to larger needles.
Next row Using yarn A, k4 [4, 4, 6, 5, 5], *inc in next st, k2 [2, 4, 1, 2, 2]; rep from * to last

Sleeve

rep of 22 sts

sizes 4 5 6   1 2 3
beg or end sts

1 2 3   4 5 6 sizes
beg or end sts

4 [4, 4, 6, 5, 5] sts, inc in next st, k to end. *57 [57, 57, 67, 67, 67] sts.*
P 1 row in A. Beg with a k row, cont in St st and patt, working from chart for sleeve, inc 1 st at each end of every row 7 [6, 5, 7, 6, 5] row until there are 75 [79, 83, 87, 91, 95] sts, working extra sts into patt. Patt 13 [10, 11, 17, 15, 19] rows straight.

1st, 2nd and 3rd sizes
Next row Using yarn A, k4 [6, 8], (inc in next st, k10) to last 5 [7, 9] sts, inc in next st, k to end. *82 [86, 90] sts.*
Next row P2 [0, 2] B, (k2A, p2B) to last 0 [2, 0] sts, k0 [2, 0] A.
Next row P0 [2, 0] A, (k2B, p2A) to last 2 [0, 2] sts, k2 [0, 2] B.

4th, 5th and 5th sizes
Next row Using yarn A, p [10, 12, 14], (inc in next st, p10) to last [11, 13, 15] sts, inc in next st, p to end. *[94, 98, 102] sts.*
Next row P [2, 0, 2] A, (k2B, p2A) to last [0, 2, 0] sts, k [0, 2, 0] B.
Next row P [0, 2, 0] B, (k2A, p2B) to last [2, 0, 2] sts, k [2, 0, 2] A.
All sizes
Rep last 2 rows until sleeve measures 17¾ [17¾, 18, 19¼, 19¾] (45 [45, 46, 49, 50]cm), ending with a wrong-side row. Using yarn A, bind off in rib.

NECKBAND

With right side of work facing, using double-pointed needles and yarn A, pick up and k 16 sts down left front neck, k18 [20, 22, 24, 26, 28] center front sts, pick up and k 16 sts up right front neck, k38 [40, 42, 44, 48, 48] center back sts. *88 [92, 96, 100, 104, 108] sts.* Divide sts onto 3 (or 4) needles. Work 5 rounds of k2B, p2A rib. Using yarn A, rib 1 round. Bind off in rib.

FINISHING

Block each piece (see page 139). Mark armhole positions 8¼ [8½, 9, 9½, 9¾, 10¼] inches (21 [22, 23, 24, 25, 26]cm) from shoulders on back and front. Sew in sleeves. Join side and sleeve seams.

Eriskay Gansey

Part of body panel A
Plain Diamond

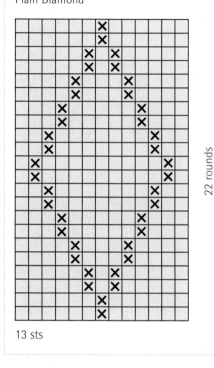

22 rounds

13 sts

Part of body panel A
Double Seed Stitch Diamond

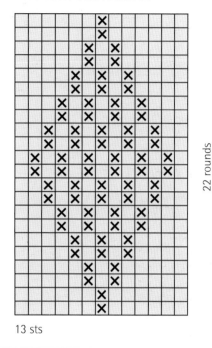

22 rounds

13 sts

✢ MATERIALS
Yarn
9 [10] x 100g (3½oz) balls Wendy
(Poppleton's) 5-ply Guernsey Wool
(100% worsted wool, approx 245 yards
[224m]) shade Cream
Needles
Circular needle size 2 (2.75mm), 32 inches
(80cm) long; set of double-pointed
needles size 2 (2.75mm); cable needle
Notions
2 [3] buttons, ⅝ inch (1.5cm) in diameter
2 stitch holders
Special abbreviation
bind 1(2)(3) Yo, knit 1(2)(3), pass over
knit yo 1(2)(3)

✢ MEASUREMENTS
Traditionally worn close-fitting
To fit chest 32–36 [38–40] inches
(81–91 [97–102]cm)
Actual chest size 36¼ [40¼] inches
(92 [102]cm)
Length from back neck 25 [26½] inches
(65 [67]cm)
Sleeve seam 18½ [21¾] inches (47 [55]cm)
Gauge
28 sts and 37 rows measure 4 inches
(10cm) over body pattern on size 2
(2.75mm) needles (or size needed to
obtain given gauge)

BODY PANEL A

Double Seed Stitch and Plain Diamonds
Repeat of 11 [13] sts
Rounds 1 and 2 K5 [6], p1, k5 [6].
Rounds 3 and 4 K4 [5], p1, k1, p1, k4 [5].
Rounds 5 and 6 K3 [4], (p1, k1) twice, p1, k3 [4].
Rounds 7 and 8 K2 [3], (p1, k1) 3 times, p1, k2 [3].
Rounds 9 and 10 K1 [2], (p1, k1) 4 times, p1, k1 [2].
2nd size only
Rounds 11 and 12 K1, (p1, k1) 6 times.
Rounds 13 and 14 K2, (p1, k1) 4 times, p1, k2.
Both sizes
Rounds 11 [15] and 12 [16] As rounds 7 and 8.
Rounds 13 [17] and 14 [18] As rounds 5 and 6.
Rounds 15 [19] and 16 [20] As rounds 3 and 4.
Rounds 17 [21] and 18 [22] As rounds 1 and 2.

1st size only
Round 19 (Bind 2) twice, yo, k3, pass yo over k3, (bind 2) twice.
2nd size only
Round 23 (Bind 2) 3 times, k1, (bind 2) 3 times.
Both sizes
Round 20 [24] Knit.
Rounds 21 [25] and 22 [26] As rounds 19 [23] and 20 [24].
Rounds 23 [27]–26 [30] As rounds 1–4.
Rounds 27 [31] and 28 [32] K3 [4], p1, k3, p1, k3 [4].
Rounds 29 [33] and 30 [34] K2 [3], p1, k5, p1, k2 [3].
Rounds 31 [35] and 32 [36] K1 [2], p1, k7, p1, k1 [2].
2nd size only
Rounds 37 and 38 K1, p1, k9, p1, k1.
Rounds 39 and 40 K2, p1, k7, p1, k2.

Both sizes
Rounds 33 [41] and 34 [42] As rounds 29 [33] and 30 [34].
Rounds 35 [43] and 36 [44] As rounds 27 [31] and 28 [32].
Rounds 37 [45] and 38 [46] As rounds 3 and 4.
Rounds 39 [47] and 40 [48] As rounds 1 and 2.
Rounds 41 [49]–44 [52] As rounds 19 [23]–22 [26].
These 44 [52] rounds form panel A.

Body panel B Marriage Lines

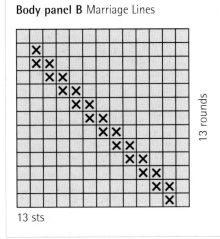

13 rounds

13 sts

Body panel C Wave

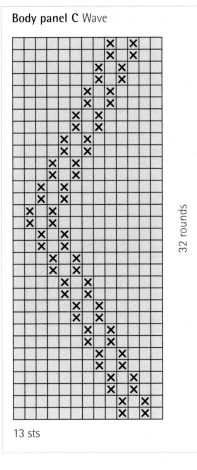

32 rounds

13 sts

Body panel D Small Starfish and Diamond

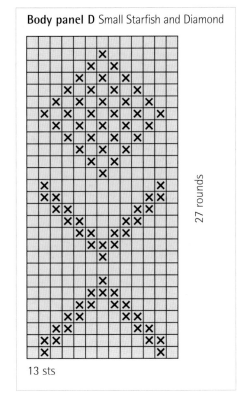

27 rounds

13 sts

BODY PANEL B

Marriage lines
Repeat of 11 [13] sts
Round 1 K1, p1, k9 [11].
Round 2 K1, p2, k8 [10].
Round 3 K2, p2, k7 [9].
Round 4 K3, p2, k6 [8].
Round 5 K4, p2, k5 [7].
Round 6 K5, p2, k4 [6].
Round 7 K6, p2, k3 [5].
Round 8 K7, p2, k2 [4].
Round 9 K8, p2, k1 [3].
2nd size only
Round 10 K9, p2, k2.
Round 11 K10, p2, k1.
Both sizes
Round 10 [12] K9 [11], p1, k1.
Round 11 [13] Knit.
These 11 [13] rounds form panel B.

BODY PANEL C

Wave
Repeat of 11 [13] sts
Rounds 1 and 2 (K1, p1) twice, k7 [9].
Rounds 3 and 4 K2, p1, k1, p1, k6 [8].
Rounds 5 and 6 K3, p1, k1, p1, k5 [7].
Rounds 7 and 8 K4, p1, k1, p1, k4 [6].
Rounds 9 and 10 K5, p1, k1, p1, k3 [5].
Rounds 11 and 12 K6, p1, k1, p1, k2 [4].
Rounds 13 and 14 K7, p1, k1, p1, k1 [3].
2nd size only
Rounds 15 and 16 K8, p1, k1, p1, k2.

Rounds 17 and 18 K9, (p1, k1) twice.
Rounds 19 and 20 As rounds 15 and 16.
Rounds 21 and 22 As rounds 13 and 14.
Both sizes
Rounds 15 [23] and 16 [24] As rounds 11 and 12.
Rounds 17 [25] and 18 [26] As rounds 9 and 10.
Rounds 19 [27] and 20 [28] As rounds 7 and 8.
Rounds 21 [29] and 22 [30] As rounds 5 and 6.
Rounds 23 [31] and 24 [32] As rounds 3 and 4.
These 24 [32] rounds form panel C.

BODY PANEL D

Small Starfish and Diamond
Repeat of 13 sts
Round 1 K1, p1, k9, p1, k1.
Round 2 K1, p2, k7, p2, k1.
Round 3 K2, p2, k5, p2, k2.
Round 4 K3, (p2, k3) twice.

Round 5 K4, p2, k1, p2, k4.
Round 6 K5, p3, k5.
Round 7 K6, p1, k6.
Round 8 Knit.
Round 9 As round 7.
Round 10 As round 6.
Round 11 As round 5.
Round 12 As round 4.
Round 13 As round 3.
Round 14 As round 2.
Round 15 As round 1.
Round 16 As round 7.
Round 17 K5, p1, k1, p1, k5.
Round 18 K4, (p1, k1) twice, p1, k4.
Round 19 K3, (p1, k1) 3 times, p1, k3.
Round 20 K2, (p1, k1) 4 times, p1, k2.
Round 21 K1, (p1, k1) 6 times.
Round 22 As round 20.
Round 23 As round 19.
Round 24 As round 18.
Round 25 As round 17.
Round 26 As round 7.
Round 27 Knit.
These 27 rounds form panel D.

YOKE PANEL E

Tree of Life, Anchor, Open Diamond
Repeat of 17 sts
Row 1 (Right side) K7, p1, k1, p1, k7.
Row 2 P6, k2, p1, k2, p6.
Row 3 K5, p2, k3, p2, k5.
Row 4 P4, k2, p5, k2, p4.
Row 5 K3, p2, k2, p1, k1, p1, k2, p2, k3.
Row 6 (P2, k2) twice, p1, (k2, p2) twice.
Row 7 K1, p2, k2, p2, k3, p2, k2, p2, k1.
Row 8 P1, k1, p2, k2, p5, k2, p2, k1, p1.
Rows 9 and 10 As rows 5 and 6.
Row 11 K2, p1, k2, p2, k3, p2, k2, p1, k2.
Rows 12 and 13 As rows 4 and 5.
Row 14 P3, k1, p2, k2, p1, k2, p2, k1, p3.
Rows 15 and 16 As rows 3 and 4.
Row 17 K4, p1, k2, p1, k1, p1, k2, p1, k4.
Rows 18 and 19 As rows 2 and 3.
Row 20 P5, (k1, p5) twice.
Rows 21 and 22 As rows 1 and 2.
Row 23 K6, p1, k3, p1, k6.
Row 24 Purl.
Row 25 As row 1.
Row 26 P7, k1, p1, k1, p7.
Row 27 (Bind 2) 4 times, bind 1, (bind 2) 4 times.
Row 28 Purl.
Rows 29 and 30 As rows 27 and 28.
Row 31 K8, p1, k8.
Row 32 P7, k3, p7.
Row 33 K6, p5, k6.
Row 34 P5, k2, p1, k1, p1, k2, p5.
Row 35 K4, p2, k2, p1, k2, p2, k4.
Row 36 P3, k2, p3, k1, p3, k2, p3.
Row 37 K2, p2, k4, p1, k4, p2, k2.
Row 38 P1, k2, p5, k1, p5, k2, p1.
Row 39 K1, p1, (k6, p1) twice, k1.
Row 40 P2, k1, p5, k1, p8.
Row 41 K8, p1, k4, p2, k2.
Row 42 P3, k2, p3, k1, p8.
Row 43 K8, p1, k2, p2, k4.
Row 44 P5, k2, p1, k1, p8.
Row 45 K8, p3, k6.
Row 46 P7, k2, p8.
Row 47 K7, p2, k8.
Row 48 P8, k3, p6.
Row 49 K5, p2, k1, p1, k8.
Row 50 P8, k1, p2, k2, p4.
Row 51 K3, p2, k3, p1, k8.
Row 52 P8, k1, p4, k2, p2.

Row 53 K1, p2, k5, p1, k8.
Row 54 P8, k1, p6, k1, p1.
Row 55 K6, p5, k6.
Row 56 P6, k5, p6.
Row 57–60 As rows 27–30.
Row 61 K6, k2 tog, yo, k1, yo, skpo, k6.
Row 62 and every foll alt row Purl.
Row 63 K5, k2 tog, yo, k3, yo, skpo, k5.
Row 65 K4, (k2 tog, yo) twice, k1, (yo, skpo) twice, k4.
Row 67 K3, (k2 tog, yo) twice, k3, (yo, skpo) twice, k3.
Row 69 K2, (k2 tog, yo) twice, k5, (yo, skpo) twice, k2.
Row 71 K4, (yo, skpo) twice, k1, (k2 tog, yo) twice, k4.
Row 73 K5, yo, skpo, yo, sl 1, k2 tog, psso, yo, k2 tog, yo, k5.
Row 75 K6, yo, skpo, k1, k2 tog, yo, k6.
Row 77 K7, yo, sl 1, k2 tog, psso, yo, k7.
Row 78 Purl.
These 78 rows form panel E.

Note: that the Open Diamond, Horseshoe, Cable, and Open Tree panel patterns are given only as line-by-line instructions.

Part of yoke panel E Tree of Life

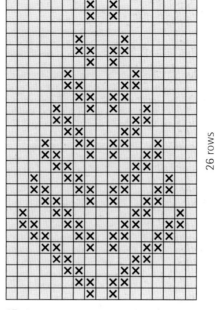

17 sts

26 rows

Part of yoke panel E Anchor

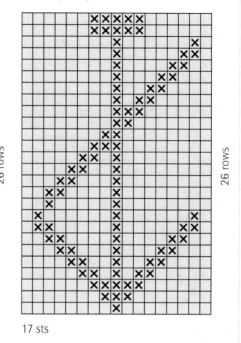

17 sts

26 rows

YOKE PANEL F

Horseshoe
Repeat of 9 [11] sts
2nd size only
Row 1 K1, yo, k3, sl 1, k2 tog, psso, k3, yo, k1.
Row 2 Purl
Both sizes
Row 1 [3] (Right side) K1 [2], yo, k2, sl 1, k2 tog, psso, k2, yo, k1 [2].
Row 2 [4] and foll alt row Purl.
Row 3 [5] K2 [3], yo, k1, sl 1, k2 tog, psso, k1, yo, k2 [3].
Row 5 [7] K3 [4], yo, sl 1, k2 tog, psso, yo, k3 [4].
Row 6 [8] Purl.
These 6 [8] rows form panel F.

YOKE PANEL G

Cable
Repeat of 6 [8] sts
Row 1 (Right side) K6 [8].
Row 2 P6 [8].
Rows 3–4 [6] Rep rows 1 and 2 once [twice].
Row 5 [7] Sl next 3 [4] sts onto cable needle

and leave at back, k3 [4], k3 [4] sts from cable needle.
Row 6 [8] As row 2.
These 6 [8] rows form panel G.

YOKE PANEL H

Starfish, Open Tree, Diamond
Repeat of 17 sts
Row 1 (Right side) K4, p1, k7, p1, k4.
Row 2 P4, k2, p5, k2, p4.

Part of yoke panel H Starfish

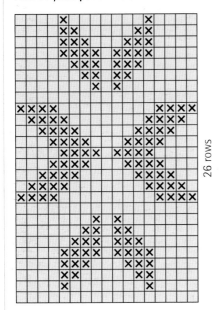

17 sts

Part of yoke panel H Diamond

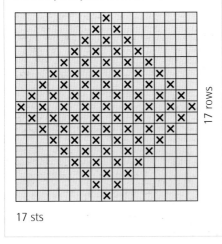

17 sts

Row 3 K4, p3, k3, p3, k4.
Row 4 P4, k4, p1, k4, p4.
Row 5 K5, p3, k1, p3, k5.
Row 6 P6, k2, p1, k2, p6.
Row 7 K7, p1, k1, p1, k7.
Row 8 Purl.
Row 9 P4, k9, p4.
Row 10 P1, k4, p7, k4, p1.
Row 11 K2, p4, k5, p4, k2.
Row 12 P3, (k4, p3) twice.
Row 13 K4, p4, k1, p4, k4.
Row 14 As row 12.
Row 15 As row 11.
Row 16 As row 10.
Row 17 As row 9.
Row 18 Purl.
Row 19 As row 7.
Row 20 As row 6.
Row 21 As row 5.
Row 22 As row 4.
Row 23 As row 3.
Row 24 As row 2.
Row 25 As row 1.
Row 26 Purl.
Row 27 (Bind 2) 4 times, bind 1, (bind 2) 4 times.
Row 28 Purl.
Rows 29 and 30 As rows 27 and 28.
Row 31 K6, k2 tog, yo, k1, yo, skpo, k6.
Row 32 and 11 foll alt rows Purl.
Row 33 K5, k2 tog, yo, k3, yo, skpo, k5.
Row 35 K4, (k2 tog, yo) twice, k1, (yo, skpo) twice, k4.
Row 37 K3, (k2 tog, yo) twice, k3, (yo, skpo) twice, k3.
Row 39 K2, (k2 tog, yo) 3 times, k1, (yo, skpo) 3 times, k2.
Row 41 K1, (k2 tog, yo) 3 times, k3, (yo, skpo) 3 times, k1.
Row 43 (K2 tog, yo) 4 times, k1, (yo, skpo) 4 times.
Row 45 As row 41.
Row 47 As row 39.
Row 49 As row 37.
Row 51 As row 35.
Row 53 As row 33.
Row 55 As row 31.
Row 56 Purl.
Rows 57–60 As rows 27–30.
Row 61 K8, p1, k8.
Row 62 P7, k1, p1, k1, p7.

Row 63 K6, (p1, k1) twice, p1, k6.
Row 64 P5, (k1, p1) 3 times, k1, p5.
Row 65 K4, (p1, k1) 4 times, p1, k4.
Row 66 P3, (k1, p1) 5 times, k1, p3.
Row 67 K2, (p1, k1) 6 times, p1, k2.
Row 68 P1, (k1, p1) 8 times.
Rows 69 and 70 Rep row 68 twice.
Row 71 As row 67.
Row 72 As row 66.
Row 73 As row 65.
Row 74 As row 64.
Row 75 As row 63.
Row 76 As row 62.
Row 77 As row 61.
Row 78 Purl.
These 78 rows form panel H.

BACK AND FRONT

This garment is knitted in one piece up to the armholes. Using circular needle, cast on 256 [280] sts. Work in rounds as follows:
Round 1 (P1, k1 tbl) to end.
Rep this round 13 times.
Next round **K31 [23], *inc in next st, k63 [45]; rep from * 0 [1] times, inc in next st, k32 [24]; rep from ** once. *260 [286] sts.*
Next round (Bind 2) to end.
Next round Knit.
Rep last 2 rounds once. Begin patt.
Round 1 *P1 [0], k1 [0], p1, work 11 [13] sts as round 1 of panel A, p1, k1, p1, work 11 [13] sts as round 1 of panel B, p1, k1, p1, work 11 [13] sts as round 1 of panel C, p1, k1, p1, work 11 [13] sts as round 1 of panel A, p1, k1, p1, work 13 sts as round 1 of panel D, p1, k1, p1, work 11 [13] sts as round 1 of panel A, p1, k1, p1, work 11 [13] sts as round 1 of panel C, p1, k1, p1, work 11 [13] sts as round 1 of panel B, p1, k1, p1, work 11 [13] sts as round 1 of panel A, p1, k1 [0]; rep from * once.
Round 2 *P1 [0], k1 [0], p1, work 11 [13] sts as round 2 of panel A, p3, work 11 [13] sts as round 2 of panel B, p3, work 11 [13] sts as round 2 of panel C, p3, work 11 [13] sts as round 2 of panel A, p3, work 13 sts as round 2 of panel D, p3, work 11 [13] sts as round 2 of panel A, p3, work 11 [13] sts as round 2 of panel C, p3, work 11 [13] sts as round 2 of panel B, p3, work 11 [13] sts as round 2 of

panel A, p1, k1 [0]; rep from * once.
These 2 rounds establish patt for body. Cont in patt as set working appropriate rounds of panels until 126 [125] rounds in all have been worked.

Shape for gusset
2nd size only
Next round *Pick up loop lying between sts and p tbl, (k1, p1) all in next st, patt 141, (p1, k1) all in next st; rep from * once.

Both sizes
Next round *P1, k1, p1, (bind 2) 61 [69] times, bind 3, p1, k1; rep from * once.

Next round *P1, k1, p1, k125 [141], p1, k1; rep from *once.

Next round *P1, k twice in next st, p1, (bind 2) 61 [69] times, bind 3, p1, k twice in next st; rep from * once.

Next round *P1, k2, p1, k125 [141], p1, k2; rep from * once.

Next round *P1, k twice in next st, k1, p1, k2, (p1, k7) 15 [17] times, p1, k2, p1, k twice in next st, k1; rep from * once.

Next round *P1, k3, p1, k3, (p1, k5, p1, k1) 15 [17] times, k2, p1, k3; rep from * once.

Next round *P1, k3, p1, k3, (p1, k5, p1, k1) 15 [17] times, k2, p1, k3; rep from * once.

Next round *P1, k1, k twice in next st, k1, p1, k4, (p1, k3) 30 [34] times, k1, p1, k twice in next st, k2; rep from * once.

Next round *P1, k4, p1, k5, (p1, k1, p1, k5) 15 [17] times, p1, k4; rep from * once.

Next round *P1, k2, k twice in next st, k1, p1, k6, (p1, k7) 14 [16] times, p1, k6, p1, k twice in next st, k3; rep from * once.

Next round *P1, k5, p1, k5, (p1, k1, p1, k5) 15 [17] times, p1, k5; rep from * once.

Next round *P1, k3, k twice in next st, k1, p1, k4, (p1, k3) 30 [34] times, k1, p1, k twice in next st, k4; rep from * once.

Next round *P1, k6, p1, k3, (p1, k5, p1, k1) 15 [17] times, k2, p1, k6; rep from * once.

Next round *P1, k4, k twice in next st, k1, p1, k2, (p1, k7) 15 [17] times, p1, k2, p1, k twice in next st, k5; rep from * once.

2nd size only
Next round *P1, k7, p1, k3, (p1, k5, p1, k1) 17 times, k2, p1, k7; rep from * once.

Next round *P1, k5, k twice in next st, k1, p1, k4, (p1, k3) 34 times, k1, p1, k twice in next st, k6; rep from * once.

Next round *P1, k8, p1, k5, (p1, k1, p1, k5) 17 times, p1, k8; rep from * once.

Next round *P1, k8, p1, k6, (p1, k7) 16 times, p1, k6, p1, k8; rep from * once.

Next round *P1, k8, p1, k5, (p1, k1, p1, k5) 17 times, p1, k8; rep from * once.

Next round *P1, k8, p1, k4 (p1, k3) 34 times, k1, p1, k8; rep from * once.

Next round *P1, k8, p1, k3, (p1, k5, p1, k1) 17 times, k2, p1, k8; rep from * once.

Next round *P1, k8, p1, k2, (p1, k7) 17 times, p1, k2, p1, k8; rep from * once.
284 [320] sts.

Both sizes
Next round *P1, k7 [8], p1, (bind 2) 61 [69] times, bind 3, p1, k7 [8]; rep from * once.

Next round **P1, k7 [8], p1, k9 [10], *inc in next st, k14 [16]; rep from * 6 times, inc in next st, k10 [11], p1, k7 [8]; rep from ** once. *300 [336] sts.*

Divide for front
Next round *P1, k7 [8], p1 and sl these 9 [10] sts onto safety pin, (bind 2) 65 [73] times, bind 3, sl next 8 [9] sts onto safety pin and turn; leave rem sts on needle.

Complete front first. Work backward and forward.

P 1 row. ***Begin yoke patt.

Row 1 K2, p9, k2 [3], p1, work 17 sts as row 1 of panel E, p1, k2 [3], p1, work 9 [11] sts as row 1 of panel F, p1, k2 [3], p1, work 6 [8] sts as row 1 of panel G, p1, k2 [3], p1, work 17 sts as row 1 of panel H, p1, k2 [3], p1, work 6 [8] sts as row 1 of panel G, p1, k2 [3], p1, work 9 [11] sts as row 1 of panel F, p1, k2 [3], p1, work 17 sts as row 1 of panel E, p1, k2 [3], p9, k2.

Row 2 P2, k9, p2 [3], k1, work 17 sts as row 2 of panel E, k1, p2 [3], k1, work 9 [11] sts as row 2 of panel F, k1, p2 [3], k1, work 6 [8] sts as row 2 of panel G, k1, p2 [3], k1, work 17 sts as row 2 of panel H, k1, p2 [3], k1, work 6 [8] sts as row 2 of panel G, k1, p2 [3], k1, work 9 [11] sts as row 2 of panel F, k1, p2 [3], k1, work 17 sts as row 2 of panel E, k1, p2 [3], k9, p2.

Row 3 K10, p1, bind 2 [3], p1, work 17 sts as row 3 of panel E, p1, bind 2 [3], p1, work 9 [11] sts as row 3 of panel F, p1, bind 2 [3], p1, work 6 [8] sts as row 3 of panel G, p1, bind 2

[3], p1, work 17 sts as row 3 panel H, p1, bind 2 [3], p1, work 6 [8] sts as row 3 of panel G, p1, bind 2 [3], p1, work 9 [11] sts as row 3 of panel F, p1, bind 2 [3], p1, work 17 sts as row 3 of panel E, p1, bind 2 [3], p1, k10.

Row 4 P10, k1, p2 [3], k1, work 17 sts as row 4 of panel E, k1, p2 [3], k1, work 9 [11] sts as row 4 of panel F, k1, p2 [3], k1, work 6 [8] sts as row 4 of panel G, k1, p2 [3], k1, work 17 sts as row 4 of panel H, k1, p2 [3], k1, work 6 [8] sts as row 4 of panel G, k1, p2 [3], k1, work 9 [11] sts as row 4 of panel F, k1, p2 [3], k1, work 17 sts as row 4 of panel E, k1, p2 [3], k1, p10. These 4 rows establish patt for yoke. Cont in patt as set, working appropriate rows of panels until 78 rows in all have been worked***.

Shape neck

Next row K2, (bind 2) 20 [23] times, k2 and turn; leave rem sts on needle. Complete left front neck first.

Next row Purl.

Row 1 K2, (bind 2) to last 2 sts, k2.
Row 2 Purl.
Row 3 K2, (purl 1, k7) to last 2 [8] sts, p1, k1 [7].
Row 4 P2 [0], (k1, p5, k1, p1) to last 2 sts, p2.
Row 5 K4, (p1, k3) to last 4 [2] sts, p1, k3 [1].
Row 6 P4 [2], (k1, p1, k1, p5) to end.
Row 7 K6, (p1, k7) to last 6 [4] sts, p1, k5 [3]. Mark end of this row.
Row 8 As row 6.
Row 9 As row 5.
Row 10 As row 4.
Row 11 As row 3.
Row 12 Purl.
Rows 13–16 Rep rows 1 and 2 twice.
Leave these sts on a spare needle. With right side of front facing, sl center 45 [49] sts onto a stitch holder, rejoin yarn to rem sts and k2, (bind 2) to last 2 sts, k2.

Next row Purl
Row 1 K2, (bind 2) to last 2 sts, k2.
Row 2 Purl.
Row 3 K1 [7], (p1, k7) to last 3 sts, p1, k2.
Row 4 P3, (k1, p5, k1, p1) to last 1 [7] sts, p1 [6], k0 [1].
Row 5 K3 [1], (p1, k3) to last st, k1.
Row 6 (P5, k1, p1, k1) to last 4 [2] sts, p4 [2].
Row 7 K5 [3], (p1, k7) to last 7 sts, p1, k6.
Row 8 As row 6.
Row 9 As row 5.

Row 10 As row 4.
Row 11 As row 3.
Row 12 Purl.
Rows 13–16 Rep rows 1 and 2 twice.
Leave these sts on a spare needle. With right side of back facing, rejoin yarn to rem sts, p1, k7 [8], p1 and sl these 9 [10] sts onto a safety pin, (bind 2) 65 [73] times, bind 3, sl last 8 [9] sts onto a safety pin. P 1 row. Work as given for front from *** to ***.

Join shoulders With right sides of back and front together, bind off 44 [50] sts, taking 1 st from each needle and working them together, sl next 45 [49] center back sts onto a stitch holder, rejoin yarn to rem sts and complete to match first shoulder.

NECKBAND

With right side facing, using circular needle and beg at marker, pick up and k 7 sts down front neck, k 45 [49] center front sts, pick up and k 10 sts up right front neck, k 45 [49] center back sts, pick up and k 5 sts to marker and 2 sts behind the first 2 picked-up sts. *114 [122] sts.*
Work backward and forward as follows:
Row 1 (Wrong side) P2, k3, (p1 tbl, k1) to last 5 sts, k3, p2.
Row 2 K5, (p1, k1 tbl) to last 5 sts, k5.
Row 3 As row 1.
Row 4 K2, bind off 2, k1 (st used in binding off) (p1, k1 tbl) to last 5 sts, k5.
Row 5 P2, k3, (p1 tbl, k1) to last 3 sts, k1, cast on 2, p2.
Rep rows 2 and 3, 4 [3] times then rows 4 and 5 once.
2nd size only
Rep last 8 rows once.
Both sizes
Rep rows 2 and 3 once. Bind off kwise.
Sew on buttons.

SLEEVES

With right side facing and using double-pointed needles, sl 9 [10] sts on safety pin onto needle, rejoin yarn and pick up and k 89 sts evenly around armhole edge, p1, k7 [8]. Work in rounds as follows:

Next round P1, k4 [5], k2 tog, k1, p91, k1, skpo, k4 [5].
Next round P1, k3 [4], k2 tog, k1, p91, k1, skpo, k3 [4].
1st size only
Next round P1, k2, k2 tog, k1, p1, k9, p2, work 11 sts as round 1 of panel B, p1, k1, p1, work 11 sts as round 1 of panel C, p1, k1, p1, work 11 sts as round 1 of panel A, p1, k1, p1, work 11 sts as round 1 of panel C, p1, k1, p1, work 11 sts as round 1 of panel B, p2, k9, p1, k1 skpo, k2.
Next round P1, k1, k2 tog, k1, p1, k9, p2, work 11 sts as round 2 of panel B, p3, work 11 sts as round 2 of panel C, p3, work 11 sts as round 2 of panel A, p3, work 11 sts as round 2 of panel C, p3, work 11 sts as round 2 of panel B, p2, k9, p1, k1, skpo, k1.
These 2 rounds establish patt.

2nd size only
Next round P1, k3, k2 tog, k1, p1, k19, p1, k1, p1, work 13 sts as round 1 of panel B, p1, k1, p1, work 13 sts as round 1 of panel A, p1, k1, p1, work 13 sts as round 1 of panel B, p1, k1, p1, k19, p1, k1, skpo, k3.
Next round P1, k2, k2 tog, k1, p1, k19, p3, work 13 sts as round 2 of panel B, p3, work 13 sts as round 2 of panel A, p3, work 13 sts as round 2 of panel B, p3, k19, p1, k1, skpo, k2.
These 2 rounds establish patt.
Next round P1, k1, k2 tog, k1, p1, patt to last 5 sts, p1, k1, skpo, k1.
Both sizes
Cont in patt as set, working appropriate rounds of panels, work as follows:
Next round P1, k1, k2 tog, p1, patt to last 4 sts, p1, skpo, k1.
Next round P1, k3, patt to last 3 sts, k3.
Rep last round 35 [39] times.
Next round P1, k1, skpo, patt to last 3 sts, k2 tog, k1. Patt 6 [7] rounds straight. Rep last 7 [8] rounds 14 times. *66 sts.*
Work another 10 [18] rounds straight.
Next round (P1, k1 tbl) to end.
Rep last round 14 times.
Bind off knitwise.

FINISHING

Block as given on page 139.

Caister Fisherman's Gansey

BACK AND FRONT

This is knitted in one piece to the armholes.
Back waistband Using circular needle, cast on 124 [132, 140, 148, 156, 164] sts. K 20 rows. Leave these sts on needle. Work front waistband as back waistband and turn.
Next round **P1, k8 [4, 8, 5, 9, 5], *inc in next st, k6 [7, 7, 8, 8, 9]; rep from * 14 times, inc in next st, k8 [5, 9, 5, 9, 6], p1**; now work from ** to ** across back waistband sts.
280 [296, 312, 328, 344, 360] sts.
Work in rounds as follows:
Round 1 *P1, k138 [146, 154, 162, 170, 178], p1; rep from * once.
Rep last round until work measures 12¼ [12½, 13, 13½, 13¾, 14¼] inches (31 [32, 33, 34, 35, 36]cm). Begin yoke patt.
Rounds 1 and 2 Purl.
Rounds 3 and 4 *P1, k138 [146, 154, 162, 170, 178], p1; rep from * once.
Rounds 5–8 As rounds 1–4.
Rounds 9 and 10 As rounds 1 and 2.
Round 11 *P1, k33 [37, 41, 45, 49, 53], (m1, k2, m1, k6) 3 times, k30, (m1, k2, m1, k6) 3 times, k27 [31, 35, 39, 43, 47], p1; rep from * once. *304 [320, 336, 352, 368, 384] sts.*
Round 12 *P3, (k2, p2) 7 [8, 9, 10, 11, 12] times,

k30, p2, (k2, p2) 7 times, k30, (p2, k2) 7 [8, 9, 10, 11, 12] times, p3; rep from * once.
Round 13 *P1, k30 [34, 38, 42, 46, 50], (p2, k6, p2) 3 times, k30, (p2, k6, p2) 3 times, k30 [34, 38, 42, 46, 50], p1; rep from * once.
Round 14 *P1, k2, (p2, k2) 7 [8, 9, 10, 11, 12] times, k32, (p2, k2) 7 times, k32, (p2, k2) 7 [8, 9, 10, 11, 12] times, p1; rep from * once.
Round 15 As round 13.
Rounds 16–23 Rep rounds 12–15 twice.
Rounds 24 and 25 As rounds 12 and 13.
Round 26 *P1, k2, (p2, k2) 7 [8, 9, 10, 11, 12] times, (k2, c6b, k2) 3 times, k2, (p2, k2) 7 times, (k2, c6b, k2) 3 times, k2, (p2, k2) 7 [8, 9, 10, 11, 12] times, p1; rep from * once.
Round 27 As round 13.
Rep rounds 12–27 once.
Divide for front
Next row P1 and sl this st onto safety pin, m1, p2, (k2, p2) 7 [8, 9, 10, 11, 12] times, k30, p2, (k2, p2) 7 times, k30, (p2, k2) 7 [8, 9, 10, 11, 12] times, p2, m1 and turn; leave rem sts on needle.
***Work backward and forward.
Row 1 (Wrong side) K1, p30 [34, 38, 42, 46, 50], (k2, p6, k2) 3 times, p30, (k2, p6, k2) 3 times, p30 [34, 38, 42, 46, 50], k1.
Row 2 K3, (p2, k2) 7 [8, 9, 10, 11, 12] times, k32, (p2, k2) 7 times, k32, (p2, k2) 7 [8, 9, 10, 11, 12] times, k1.
Row 3 As row 1.
Row 4 K1, p2, (k2, p2) 7 [8, 9, 10, 11, 12] times, k30, p2, (k2, p2) 7 times, k30, (p2, k2) 7 [8, 9, 10, 11, 12] times, p2, k1.
Rows 5–12 Rep rows 1–4 twice.
Row 13 As row 1.
Row 14 K3, (p2, k2) 7 [8, 9, 10, 11, 12] times, (k2, c6b, k2) 3 times, k2 (p2, k2) 7 times, (k2, c6b, k3) 3 times, k2, (p2, k2) 7 [8, 9, 10, 11, 12] times, k1.
Row 15 As row 1.
Row 16 As row 4.
These 16 rows form patt. Cont in patt until armholes measure 6¾ [7, 7½, 8, 8¼, 8¾] inches (17 [18, 19, 20, 21, 22]cm), ending with a wrong-side row.
Next row Patt 33 [37, 41, 45, 49, 53], (k2 tog, k1, k2 tog, k5) 3 times, patt 30, (k2 tog, k1,

k2 tog, k5) 3 times, patt 29 [33, 37, 41, 45, 49]. 140 [148, 156, 164, 172, 180] sts***.
Next row K1, p to last st, k1.
Shape neck
Next row Patt 46 [49, 52, 55, 58, 61] sts and turn; leave rem sts on needle.
Complete left front neck first.

✢ MATERIALS
Yarn
7 [7, 8, 9, 9, 10] x 100g balls Frangipani 5-ply Guernsey wool (100% wool, approx 245 yards [225m], shade Sea Spray (also available in 500g [17½oz] cones, approx 1240 yards [1,130m])
Needles
1 circular needle size 2 (3mm), 32 inches (80cm) long
1 set double-pointed needles size 2 (3mm)
1 cable needle
Notions
2 stitch holders
Special abbreviations
m1 Pick up loop lying between sts and k tbl
c6b Sl next 3 sts onto cable needle and leave at back of work, k3 from left-hand needle, k3 from cable needle

✢ MEASUREMENTS
To fit chest 34 [36, 38, 40, 42, 44] inches (87 [91, 97, 102, 107, 112]cm)
Actual chest size 39¼ [41¾, 43¾, 46, 48, 50¼] inches
(100 [106, 111, 117, 122 128]cm)
Length from back neck 22½ [23, 24, 24¾, 25½, 26¼] inches
(57 [59, 61, 63, 65, 67]cm)
Sleeve seam 17 [17¼, 17¾, 18, 18½, 19] inches (43 [44, 45, 46, 47, 48]cm)
Gauge
28 sts and 36 rows measure 4 inches (10cm) over stockinette stitch on size 2 (3mm) needles (or size needed to obtain given gauge)

Chest bands and seed stitch

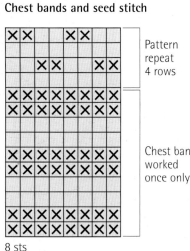

Pattern repeat 4 rows

Chest bands worked once only

8 sts

Row 1 Purl.
Rows 2 and 3 Knit.
Row 4 Purl.
Rep these 4 rows 5 times then rows 1 and 2 once. Leave these sts on spare needle. With right side of front facing, sl center 48 [50, 52, 54, 56, 58] sts onto stitch holder, rejoin yarn to rem sts and p to end. Complete to match left front neck.

With right side of back facing, rejoin yarn to rem sts, p1 and sl this st onto safety pin, m1, p2, (k2, p2) 7 [8, 9, 10, 11, 12] times, k30, p2, (k2, p2) 7 times, k30, (p2, k2) 7 [8, 9, 10, 11, 12] times, p2, m1. Work as given for front from *** to ***.

Join shoulders
With right sides of back and front together, bind off 46 [49, 52, 55, 58, 61] sts taking 1 st from each needle and working them tog. Sl next 48 [50, 52, 54, 56, 58] center back sts onto stitch holder, rejoin yarn to rem sts and complete to match first shoulder.

NECKBAND

With right side facing, using double-pointed needles, pick up and k 18 sts down left front neck, k across 48 [50, 52, 54, 56, 58] center front sts, pick up and k 18 sts up right front neck and k across 48 [50, 52, 54, 56, 58] center back sts. *132 [136, 140, 144, 148, 152] sts.*

Work 12 rounds in K1, p1, rib. Bind off in rib.

SLEEVES

With right side facing, using double-pointed needles, p1 from safety pin, pick up and k 108 [116, 120, 128, 132, 140] sts evenly around armhole edge, then p1 from safety pin. Work in rounds as follows:
Round 1 P1, k to last st, p1.
Round 2 P1, skpo, k to last 3 sts, k2 tog, p1.
Rep last 2 rounds 4 times.
Begin band patt.
Round 1 Purl.
Round 2 P1, k to last st, p1.
Round 3 P3, (k2, p2) to last st, p1.
Round 4 As round 2.
Round 5 P1, (k2, p2) to last 3 sts, k2, p1.
Rounds 6 and 7 As rounds 2 and 3.
Round 8 P1, skpo, k to last 3 sts, k2 tog, p1.
Round 9 P1, k1, (p2, k2) to last 4 sts, p2, k1, p1.
Round 10 As round 2.
Round 11 P2, (k2, p2) to end.
Round 12 As round 2.

Round 13 As round 9.
Round 14 As round 8.
Round 15 P1, k2, (p2, k2) to last st, p1.
Round 16 As round 2.
Round 17 Purl.
Next round P1, k to last st, p1.
Rep this round once.
Next round P1, skpo, k to last 3 sts, k2 tog, p1.
Next round P1, k to last st, p1.
Rep last round 4 [3, 3, 2, 2, 2] times.
Rep last 6 [5, 5, 4, 4, 4] rounds until 62 [62, 64, 64, 66, 68] sts rem, ending with dec round. Cont straight until sleeve measures 14¼ [14½, 15, 15¼, 15¾, 16] inches (36 [37, 38, 39, 40, 41]cm), ending 1 st before end of last round.
Next round P2 tog, k9 [9, 10, 10, 9, 8], *k2 tog, k8 [8, 8, 8, 9, 6]; rep from * to last 11 [11, 12, 12, 11, 10] sts, k2 tog, k to end.
56 [56, 58, 58, 60, 60] sts.
Work 2¾ inches (7cm) in rounds of k1, p1 rib. Bind off in rib.

FINISHING

Block as given on page 139.

Fair Isle

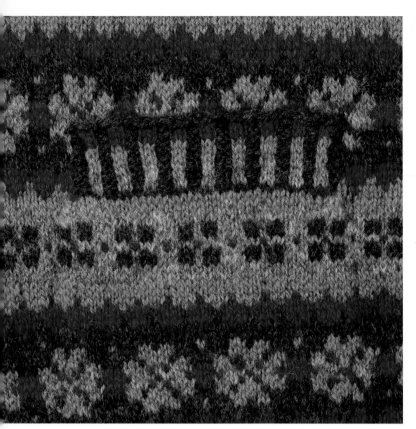

The Shetland Islands, which include tiny Fair Isle, have always been a thriving center for traders and fishermen, as they have a large, safe harbor at Lerwick, sheltered by the island of Bressay. Many sea routes converged on Shetland over the centuries, and the harbor was a haven for hundreds of ships of all nationalities in their journey from the south of Europe to the Baltic, Scandinavia, the Faroe Islands, and Iceland.

It is difficult to ascertain the exact origins of Fair Isle patterns, but they seem to be related to patterns found in Estonia and Russia and could easily have been brought to Shetland by traders. There is a romantic tale that the islanders copied the patterns from those worn by sailors of the Spanish Armada ship El Gran Griffon, which was wrecked on Fair Isle in 1588. Since this story seems to have originated in the middle of the nineteenth century, it seems more likely that the knitters were using a myth to boost the sale of their knitting to visitors.

The earliest examples of Fair Isle patterned knitting as we know it today, are a beautiful cap and coin purse dating from 1850, which can be seen in the National Museum of Antiquities of Scotland, in Edinburgh. These have large geometric patterns in colored bands, and are knitted in silk; it is possible they were made for the Victorian tourist trade to the islands. The patterns of the mid-nineteenth-century Fair Isle knitting often consist of large hexagonal shapes with different crosses and motifs within them; these are described as OXO patterns. In between are different small-or "peerie"-patterns, each one having a different background color.

The ingenuity of the individual knitters produced led a large variety of patterns; and some knitters would pride themselves on never using the same one twice within a garment. All their designs are achieved by using just two colors of yarn in any one row, with the color not in use at a given time being stranded along the back of the knitting. The resulting double thickness gives the fabric increased warmth.

The colors originally used were the natural shades of the sheep's wool, ranging from natural black through all the grays, browns, and fawns to the natural creamy white. Shetland sheep come in many different colors, unlike other breeds, and the colors have wonderful Shetland names—"shaela" and "sholmit" (shades of gray); "eesit" and "mooskit" (shades of fawn); "mogit" and "moorit" (shades of brown). The dyed colors were originally obtained from natural dyes, with madder providing red, indigo giving blue, and onion skin making a yellow-gold color. The madder and indigo were imported, and were first used in Shetland around 1840. These were the colors used in all Fair Isle knitting until about 1920, when mill-dyed yarns from Scotland began to be more generally used.

Around 1900, the first allover-patterned Fair Isle sweaters appeared; until that time, the knitters were producing smaller items such as scarves, hats, gloves, and stockings. These sweaters were seamless garments, knitted in the round, with the sleeves knitted down from the shoulder to the cuff, and were used as work wear by the local fishermen. However, a chance act resulted in the growth of a thriving industry.

In 1922, the knitters of Shetland sent a parcel of knitwear to Princess Mary, daughter of George V, on the occasion of her marriage. Apparently the parcel included a Fair Isle-patterned sweater, which came into the hands of her brother Edward, the Prince of Wales (later Edward VIII and Duke of Windsor). The Prince wore the sweater at the Royal and Ancient Golf Club of St. Andrews, and he then had his portrait painted by Sir Henry Lander wearing it. Fair Isle knitwear immediately became highly fashionable, and it remained popular into the 1940s

Here you will find traditional patterns on three vests and two pullovers. One of the sweaters uses the natural Shetland colors and is knitted in the round; the other has a modern colorway using double knitting yarn, for those who want to produce a slightly heavier sweater. These old patterns make classic garments that will give years of pleasure and attract admiration wherever they are seen.

Cross and Flower Fair Isle Crewneck

A traditional pattern takes on a new, bolder look when double knitting yarn, in soft woodland shades, is used. Knitted in separate pieces and then seamed, this makes a warm sweater for either a man or a woman. The OXO pattern is complemented by striped ribbing.

Cross and Square Fair Isle Vest

This sleeveless vest combines a bold, traditional pattern—a repeating cross motif—with more contemporary colors and would suit either a man or a woman. It is knitted in the round in the Shetland way, which means that the pattern is always facing you as you work.

Diamond Fair Isle Vest

A pretty vest in a traditional pattern uses a modern color scheme in lovely, soft moorland shades of Shetland wool, but another lightweight yarn could be used. The pattern of "shaded diamonds," or "peaks," was very popular in the Fair Isle knitting of the 1940s.

Katie's Fair Isle Vest

This old, intricate pattern uses the authentic Fair Isle colors of madder red and indigo blue and has rows of OXO, the Armada cross, and "peerie" (little) patterns in between. It has become known as "Katie's" pattern, after the knitter, and makes a slipover that is also suitable for men.

OXO Fair Isle Crewneck

This beautiful old pattern was taken from a sweater owned by Margaret Stuart's grandmother, dating from about 1915. All the natural shades of the Shetland wool are used in the bold pattern. The striped ribbing, like the seamless construction, is another feature of real Fair Isle.

Cross and Flower Fair Isle Crewneck

❊ MATERIALS

Yarn
Rowan pure wool DK (approx 136 yards [125m])
A 2 [2, 2, 3, 3] x 50g (1¾oz) balls, shade 020 Parsley; B 2 [2, 2, 3, 3] x 50g (1¾oz) balls, shade 021 Glade; C 2 [2, 2, 3, 3] x 50g (1¾oz) balls, shade 015 Barley; D 2 [3, 3, 3, 3] x 50g (1¾oz) balls, shade 016 Hessian
E 2 [2, 2, 2, 3] x 50g (1¾oz) balls, shade 035 Quarry; F 3 [3, 3, 3, 4] x 50g (1¾oz) balls, shade 007 Cypress

Needles
1 pair size 5 (3.75mm); 1 pair size 7 (4.5mm)

Notions
1 stitch holder

Special abbreviation
m1 Pick up loop lying between sts and k tbl

❊ MEASUREMENTS

To fit chest 34 [36, 38, 40, 42] inches (86 [91, 97, 102, 107]cm)
Actual chest size 37¾ [40, 41¾, 43¼, 45½] inches (96 [102, 106, 110, 116]cm)
Length to back neck 21½ [23¼, 23½, 24¼, 25½] inches (55 [59, 60, 62, 65]cm)
Sleeve seam 16 [16½, 17¾, 19, 19¾] inches (41 [42, 45, 48, 50]cm)

Gauge
23 sts and 26 rows measure 4 inches (10cm) over pattern on size 7 (4.5mm) needles (or size needed to obtain given gauge)
Note: The motif that falls in the center of the body and sleeves may vary from the photograph depending on the size knitted.

BACK

Carry yarn not in use loosely across wrong side of work. Using smaller needles and yarn A, cast on 106 [110, 114, 118, 122] sts.

Row 1 (Right side) P2A, (k2B, p2A) to end.
Row 2 K2A, (p2B, k2A) to end.
Row 3 P2A, (k2C, p2A) to end.
Row 4 K2A, (p2C, k2A) to end.
Row 5 P2A, (k2D, p2A) to end.
Row 6 K2A, (p2D, k2A) to end.
Row 7 P2A, (k2E, p2A) to end.
Row 8 K2A, (p2E, k2A) to end.
Row 9 P2A, (k2F, p2A) to end.
Row 10 K2A, (p2F, k2A) to end.
Rows 11 and 12 As rows 7 and 8.
Rows 13 and 14 As rows 5 and 6.
Rows 15 and 16 As rows 3 and 4.
Rows 17 and 18 As rows 1 and 2.
Change to larger needles.
Next row Using yarn A, k5 [7, 9, 9, 7], *m1, k16 [12, 12, 10, 9]; rep from * to last 5 [7, 9, 9, 7] sts, m1, k to end. *113 [119, 123, 129, 135] sts.*
P 1 row in A. Reading odd-numbered (k) rows from right to left and even-numbered (p) rows from left to right, cont in St st and patt from chart until work measures 13¾ [14½, 15, 15¾, 15¾] inches (35 [37, 38, 40, 40]cm), ending with a wrong-side row.
Shape armholes
Bind off 12 [14, 14, 16, 16] sts at beg of next 2 rows. *89 [91, 95, 97, 103] sts.* Cont straight in patt until armholes measure 8 [8¾, 8¾, 8¾, 9¾] inches (20 [22, 22, 22, 25]cm), ending with a wrong-side row.
Shape shoulders
Next row Bind off 25 [25, 27, 27, 30] sts, patt to last 25 [25, 27, 27, 30] sts. Bind off these sts. Leave rem 39 [41, 41, 43, 43] sts on a spare needle.

FRONT

Work as given for back until armholes measure 4 [4¼, 4¼, 4¼, 5] inches (10 [11, 11, 11, 13]cm), ending with a wrong-side row.
Shape neck
Next row Patt 38 [38, 40, 41, 44] sts and turn; leave rem sts on a spare needle. Complete left side of neck first. Bind off 2 sts at beg of next row and foll 3 alt rows, then 1 st on every alt row until 25 [25, 27, 27, 30] sts rem. Cont straight until front matches back to shoulder, ending with a wrong-side row. Bind off. With right side facing, sl center 13 [15, 15, 15, 15] sts onto stitch holder, rejoin appropriate yarn to rem sts and patt to end. Patt 1 row. Complete to match first side of neck.

SLEEVES

Using smaller needles and yarn A, cast on 46 [46, 46, 50, 54] sts. Work 18 rows in rib as given for back waistband. Change to larger needles.
Next row Using A, k5 [7, 7, 7, 6], *m1, k3 [2, 2, 2, 3]; rep from * to last 2 [5, 5, 5, 3] sts, k to end. *59 [63, 63, 69, 69] sts.*
P 1 row in A. Cont in St st and patt from chart as given for 2nd [3rd, 3rd, 4th, 4th] sizes, inc 1 st at each end of row 9 [1, 9, 9, 3] and every foll row 4 [4, 4, 5, 5] until there are 95 [103, 103, 103, 117] sts, working extra sts into patt. Cont straight until sleeve measures 16 [16½, 17¾, 19, 19¾] inches (41 [42, 45, 48, 50]cm). Mark each end of last row. Work 2 [2¼, 2¼, 2¾, 2¾] inches (5 [6, 6, 7, 7]cm) in patt, ending with a wrong-side row. Bind off.

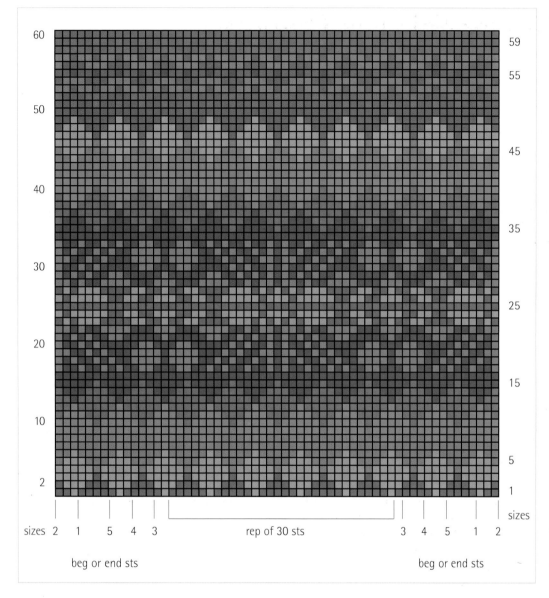

60 — 59
55
50
45
40 — 45
35
30 — 25
20 — 15
10
5
2 — 1

sizes 2 1 5 4 3 | rep of 30 sts | 3 4 5 1 2 sizes

beg or end sts   beg or end sts

NECKBAND

Join right shoulder seam. With right side facing, using smaller needles and yarn A, pick up and k 23 [25, 27, 28, 30] sts down left side neck, k across 13 [15, 15, 15, 15] center front sts, pick up and k 23 [25, 27, 28, 30] sts up right side neck, k across 39 [41, 41, 43, 43] center back sts. *98 [106, 110, 114, 118] sts.* **Next row** (Wrong side) K2A, (p2D, k2A) to end. Now rep rows 13 and 18 as given for back waistband. Using A, bind off in rib.

FINISHING

Block each piece as given on page 139. Join left shoulder and neckband seam. Sew in sleeves, sewing rows above markers to bound-off sts at armholes. Join side and sleeve seams.

Key

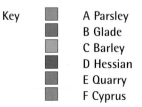

A Parsley
B Glade
C Barley
D Hessian
E Quarry
F Cyprus

Cross and Square Fair Isle Vest

❉ **MATERIALS**

Yarn

Jamieson's Spindrift 2-ply (100% Shetland wool, approx 115 yards [105m])

A 4 [4, 4, 4] x 25g (⁹⁄₁₀oz) balls, shade 730 Dark Navy; C 2 [2, 2, 2] x 25g (⁹⁄₁₀oz) balls, shade 577 Chestnut; E 1 [1, 2, 2] x 25g (⁹⁄₁₀oz) balls, shade 763 Pacific; F 3 [3, 4, 4] x 25g (⁹⁄₁₀oz) balls, shade 179 Buttermilk

Jamieson and Smith's 2-ply Jumper Weight (100% Shetland wool, approx 125 yards [115m])

B 1 [1, 2, 2] x 25g (⁹⁄₁₀oz) balls, shade FC14 (purple mix); D 1 [1, 2, 2] x 25g (⁹⁄₁₀oz) balls, shade 4 (moorit brown); G 1 [1, 2, 2] x 25g (⁹⁄₁₀oz) balls, shade 128 (red mix)

Needles

1 circular needle size 1 (2.75mm), 24 inches (60cm) long; 1 circular needle size 1 (2.75mm), 16 inches (40cm) long; 1 circular needle size 2 (3mm), 32 inches (80cm) long

Special abbreviation

m1 Pick up loop lying between sts and k tbl

❉ **MEASUREMENTS**

To fit chest 34 [36, 38, 40] inches (86 [91, 97, 102]cm)

Actual chest size 38¼ [39¾, 43, 45¾] inches (97 [101, 109, 116]cm)

Length from back neck 21¾ [22¾, 24, 24¾] inches (55 [58, 61, 63]cm)

Gauge

33 sts and 38 rows measure 4 inches (10cm) over pattern on 3mm needles (or size needed to obtain given gauge)

BACK AND FRONT

This garment is knitted in one piece to the armholes. Carry yarn not in use loosely across wrong side of work. Using smaller circular needle 24 inches (60cm) long and yarn A, cast on 276 [300, 320, 336] sts. Cont in rounds as follows:

Rounds 1–3 (K2B, p2A) to end.

Rounds 4–6 (K2C, p2A) to end.

Rounds 7–9 (K2D, p2A) to end.

Rounds 10–12 (K2E, p2A) to end.

Rounds 13–15 As rounds 7–9.

Rounds 16–18 As rounds 4–6.

Rounds 19–21 As rounds 1–3.

Change to larger circular needle.

Next round Using A, *(k8, m1) 2 [2, 1, 1] times, k7 [9, 8, 6], m1; rep from * to end. *312 [336, 360, 384] sts.*

Reading rounds from right to left cont in St st and patt from chart.

Cont in patt until work measures 13¾ [13¾, 15, 15] inches (35 [35, 38, 38]cm), ending 1 [7, 14, 20] sts before end of last round.

Divide for back and front

Next round *Bind off 21 [21, 23, 23], patt 135 [147, 157, 169] including st used in binding off; rep from * once.

Complete back first. Keeping continuity of patt, work backward and forward in St st, reading p rows from left to right from chart.

Next row Patt to end.

Next row K1, skpo, patt to last 3 sts, k2 tog, k1.

Rep last 2 rows until 109 [117, 127, 137] sts rem.

Next 3 rows Patt to end.

Next row K1, skpo, patt to last 3 sts, k2 tog, k1.

Rep last 4 rows 5 times. *97 [105, 115, 125] sts.*

Cont straight until armhole measures 8 [9, 9, 9¾] inches (20 [23, 23, 25]cm), ending with a wrong-side row.

Shape shoulders

Next row Bind off 30 [32, 35, 40] sts, patt to last 30 [32, 35, 40] sts, bind off these sts. Leave rem 37 [41, 45, 45] sts on a spare needle. With wrong side of front facing, rejoin appropriate yarn to rem sts.

Next row Patt 67 [73, 78, 84] sts and turn; leave rem sts on needle.

Complete right side of neck first.

Next row Skpo, patt to last 3 sts, k2 tog, k1.

Next row Patt to end.

Rep last 2 rows 4 [4, 4, 5] times.

Next row Patt to last 3 sts, k2 tog, k1.

Next row Patt to end.

Next row Skpo, patt to last 3 sts, k2 tog, k1.

Next row Patt to end.

Rep last 4 rows 3 [4, 4, 4] times.

Next 2 rows Patt to end.

Next row Skpo, patt to last 3 sts, k2 tog, k1.

Next row Patt to end.

Rep last 4 rows 5 times. Keeping armhole edge straight, cont to dec at neck edge as before until 30 [32, 35, 40] sts rem. Cont straight until front matches back to shoulder, ending with a wrong-side row.

Bind off.

With wrong side of front facing, sl next st onto safety pin, rejoin appropriate yarn to rem sts and patt to end.

Next row K1, skpo, patt to last 2 sts, k2 tog.

Main colour combination

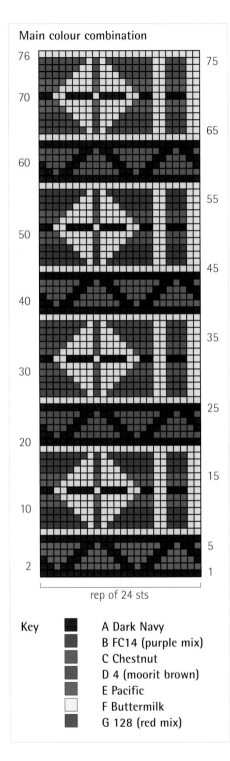

76 75
70
65
60
55
50
45
40
35
30
25
20
15
10 5
2 1

rep of 24 sts

Key

A Dark Navy
B FC14 (purple mix)
C Chestnut
D 4 (moorit brown)
E Pacific
F Buttermilk
G 128 (red mix)

Next row Patt to end.
Rep last 2 rows 4 [4, 4, 5] times.
Next row K1, skpo, patt to end.
Next row Patt to end.

Next row K1, skpo, patt to last 2 sts, k2 tog.
Next row Patt to end.
Rep last 4 rows 3 [4, 4, 4] times.
Next 2 rows Patt to end.
Next row K1, skpo, patt to last 2 sts, k2 tog.
Next row Patt to end.
Complete as given for right side of neck.

NECKBAND

Join shoulder seams. With right side facing, using smaller circular needle 24 inches (40cm) long and yarn A, pick up and k 76 [84, 84, 88] sts down left side neck, k center front st, pick up and k 76 [84, 84, 88] sts up right side of neck, k 18 [20, 22, 22] inc in next st, k 18 [20, 22, 22] across center back sts. *191 [211, 215, 223] sts.*
Round 1 (K2D, p2A) 18 [20, 20, 21] times, k2D, using A, skpo, k1, k2 tog, (k2D, p2A) 28 [31, 32, 33] times.
Round 2 (K2D, p2A) 18 [20, 20, 21] times, using D, k1, skpo, k1A, using D, k2 tog, k1D, p2A, (k2D, p2A) 27 [30, 31, 32] times.
Round 3 (K2D, p2A) 18 [20, 20, 21] times, using D, skpo, k1A, using D, k2 tog, p2A, (k2D, p2A) 27 [30, 31, 32] times.
Round 4 (K2C, p2A) 17 [19, 19, 20] times, k2C, using A, p1, yb, skpo, k1, k2 tog, p1, (k2C, p2A) 27 [30, 31, 32] times.
Round 5 (K2C, p2A) 17 [19, 19, 20] times, k2C, using A, skpo, k1, k2 tog, (k2C, p2A) 27

[30, 31, 32] times.
Round 6 K2C, p2A) 17 [19, 19, 20] times, using C, k1, skpo, k1A, using C, k2 tog, k1C, p2A, (k2C, p2A) 26 [29, 30, 31] times.
Round 7 (K2B, p2A) 17 [19, 19, 20] times, using B, skpo, k1A, using B, k2 tog, p2A, (k2B, p2A) 26 [29, 30, 31] times.
Round 8 (K2B, p2A) 16 [18, 18, 19] times, k2B, using A, p1, yb, skpo, k1, k2 tog, p1, (k2B, p2A) 26 [29, 30, 31] times.
Round 9 (K2B, p2A) 16 [18, 18, 19] times, k2B, using A, skpo, k1, k2 tog, (k2B, p2A) 26 [29, 30, 31] times.
Using A, bind off in rib.

ARMBANDS

With right side facing, using smaller circular needle 16 inches (40cm) long, yarn A and beg at center of bound-off sts at armhole, pick up and k 156 [168, 172, 184] sts evenly around armhole edge. Work in rounds as follows:
Rounds 1–3 (K2D, p2A) to end.
Rounds 4–6 (K2C, p2A) to end.
Rounds 7–9 (K2B, p2A) to end.
Using A, bind off in rib.

FINISHING

Darn in any loose ends. Block as given on page 139.

Diamond Fair Isle Vest

❋ MATERIALS

Yarn

Jamieson and Smith's 2-ply Jumper Weight (100% Shetland wool, approx 125 yards [115m]) A 4 [4, 5, 5] x 25g (⁹⁄₁₀oz) balls, shade FC14 (purple mix); C 3 [3, 4, 4] x 25g (⁹⁄₁₀oz) balls, shade 141 (clan gray); D 3 [3, 4, 4] x 25g (⁹⁄₁₀oz) balls, shade FC64 (fawn mix)

Jamieson's Spindrift 2-ply (100% Shetland wool, approx 115 yards [105m]) B 3 [3, 4, 4] x 25g (⁹⁄₁₀oz) balls, shade 577 Chestnut

Needles

1 pair size 1 (2.75mm); 1 pair size 2 (3mm); 1 circular needle size 1 (2.75mm), 32 inches (80cm) long; 1 circular needle size 1 (2.75mm), 24 inches (40cm) long; 1 circular needle size 2 (3mm), 32 inches (80cm) long

Notions

5 buttons, ⅝ inch (1.5cm) in diameter
2 stitch holders

❋ MEASUREMENTS

To fit chest 34 [36, 38, 40] inches (86 [91, 97, 102]cm)

Actual chest size 38¼ [41¼, 44, 46¾] inches (97 [105, 112, 119]cm)

Length from back neck 22 [23¼, 24½, 25¼] inches (56 [59, 62, 64]cm)

Gauge

33 sts and 38 rows measure 4 inches (10cm) over pattern on size 2 (3mm) needles (or size needed to obtain given gauge)

POCKET LININGS

Carry yarn not in use loosely across wrong side of work. Using larger pair of needles and yarn A, cast on 37 sts. Purl 1 row in D.

Reading odd-numbered (k) rows from right to left and even-numbered (p) rows from left to right and beg with a k row, cont in St st, work 36 rows from chart 2. Leave these sts on a spare needle. Make another pocket lining to match.

MAIN PART

Using smaller circular needle 32 inches (80cm) long and A, cast on 310 [334, 358, 382] sts. Work backward and forward as follows:

Row 1 (Right side) K2B, (p2A, k2B) to end.
Row 2 P2B, (k2A, p2B) to end.
Rows 3 and 4 As rows 1 and 2.
Row 5 K2C, (p2A, k2B) to end.
Row 6 P2C, (k2A, p2C) to end.
Rows 7 and 8 As rows 5 and 6.
Row 9 K2D, (p2A, k2D) to end.
Row 10 P2D, (k2A, p2D) to end.
Rows 11 and 12 As rows 9 and 10.
Rows 13–16 As rows 5–8.
Rows 17–20 As rows 1–4.
Change to larger circular needle. K 1 row in A, inc 3 sts evenly. 313 [337, 361, 385] sts.
P 1 row in D. Cont in St st and patt from chart 1, work 36 rows.
Place pocket

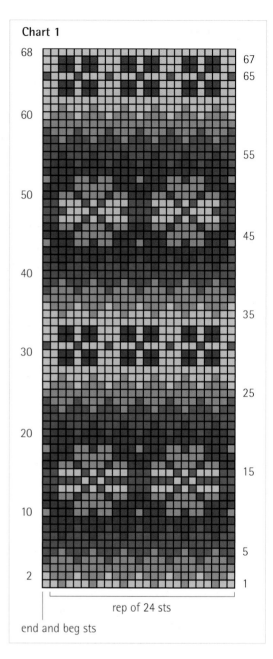

Chart 1

rep of 24 sts

end and beg sts

Next row Patt 25 sts, sl next 37 sts onto stitch holder, patt across first pocket lining, patt to last 62 sts, sl next 37 sts onto stitch holder, patt across second pocket lining, patt to end. Cont in patt until work measures 13¾ [13¾, 15, 15] inches (35 [35, 38, 38]cm), ending with a wrong-side row.
Divide for armholes
Next row Patt 66 [72, 75, 81] sts, bind off 20 [20, 24, 24], patt 141 [153, 163, 175] sts

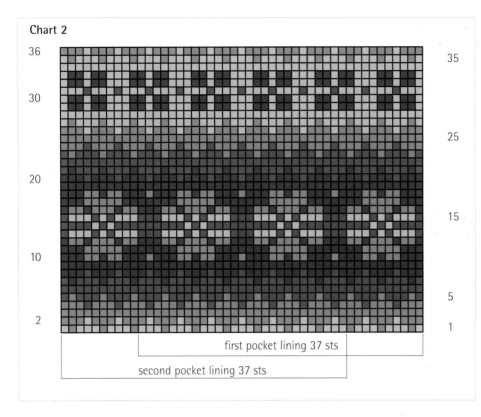

Chart 2

first pocket lining 37 sts

second pocket lining 37 sts

using smaller circular needle 32 inches (80cm) long and yarn A, pick up and k 112 [112, 120, 120] sts up right front to front shaping, 73 [82, 82, 90] sts up shaped edge to shoulder, k 32 [35, 37, 39], k2 tog, k 31 [34, 36, 38] across back neck sts, pick up and k 73 [82, 82, 90] sts down shaped edge of left front and 112 [112, 120, 120] sts down left front. *434 [458, 478, 498] sts.* Work backward and forward as follows:

Row 1 (Wrong side) P2D, (k2A, p2D) to end.

Row 2 K2D, (p2A, k2D) to end.

Row 3 As row 1.

The last 2 rows form rib. Using C instead of D, cont in rib.

Row 4 Rib 4, *bind off 2, rib 24 [24, 26, 26]; rep from * 4 times, rib to end.

Row 5 Rib to end, casting on 2 sts over those bound off in previous row. Rib 1 row. Using B instead of D, rib 3 rows. Using A, bind off in rib.

including st used in binding off, bind off 20 [20, 24, 24], patt to end.
Complete left front first. Keep continuity of patt.

Next row Patt to end.

Next row K1, skpo, patt to last 2 sts, k2 tog.
Rep last 2 rows 4 [5, 5, 5] times.

Next row Patt to end.

Next row Patt to last 2 sts, k2 tog.

Next row Patt to end.

Next row K1, skpo, patt to last 2 sts, k2 tog.
Rep last 4 rows 3 times. Keeping armhole edge straight, cont dec at neck edge as set on every foll alt row until 35 [39, 42, 47] sts rem, then on every foll row 4 until 29 [31, 34, 38] sts rem. Cont straight until armhole measures 8 [9, 9, 9¾] inches (20 [23, 23, 25]cm), ending at armhole edge.

Shape shoulder

Bind off 10 [10, 11, 13] sts at beg of next row and foll alt row. Work 1 row. Bind off rem 9 [11, 12, 12] sts.
With wrong side facing, rejoin appropriate yarn to 141 [153, 163, 175] sts for back.

Next row Patt to end.

Next row K1, skpo, patt to last 3 sts, k2 tog, k1.

Rep last 2 rows 4 [5, 5, 5] times.

Next 3 rows Patt to end.

Next row K1, skpo, patt to last 3 sts, k2 tog, k1.
Rep last 4 rows 3 times. *123 [133, 143, 155] sts.*
Cont straight until armholes measure 8 [9, 9, 9¾] inches (20 [23, 23, 25]cm), ending with a wrong-side row.

Shape shoulders

Bind off 10 [10, 11, 13] sts at beg of next 4 rows and 9 [11, 12, 12] sts at beg of foll 2 rows.
Leave rem 65 [71, 75, 79] sts on a spare needle.
With wrong side facing, rejoin appropriate yarn to rem 66 [72, 75, 81] sts for right front.

Next row Patt to end.

Next row Skpo, patt to last 3 sts, k2 tog, k1.
Rep last 2 rows 4 [5, 5, 5] times.

Next row Patt to end.

Next row Skpo, patt to end.

Next row Patt to end.

Next row Skpo, patt to last 3 sts, k2 tog, k1.
Complete as given for left front.

BUTTON BAND

Join shoulder seams. With right side facing,

ARMBANDS

With right side facing, using smaller circular needle 16 inches (40cm) long, yarn A and beg at center of bound-off sts for armhole, pick up and k 156 [172, 172, 184] sts evenly around armhole edge. Work in rounds as follows:

Rounds 1–3 (K2D, p2A) to end.

Rounds 4–6 (K2C, p2A) to end.

Rounds 7–9 (K2B, p2A) to end.
Using A, bind off in rib.

POCKET EDGINGS

With right side facing, using smaller pair of needles, rejoin yarn A to the 37 sts on pocket top. K 1 row, inc 1 st at center. *38 sts.*
Work 9 rows in rib as given for front band, omitting buttonholes. Using A, bind off in rib.

FINISHING

Darn in any lose ends. Block as given on page 139. Stitch down pocket linings and sides of pocket edgings. Sew on buttons.

Katie's Fair Isle Vest

❋ MATERIALS

Yarns

Jamieson's Spindrift 2-ply (100% Shetland wool, approx 115 yards [105m])

A 4 [4, 4, 4, 4] x 25g (⁹/₁₀oz) balls, shade 726 Prussian Blue; B 2 [2, 2, 2, 2] x 25g (⁹/₁₀oz) balls, shade 289 Fool's Gold; D 2 [2, 2, 2, 2] x 25g (⁹/₁₀oz) balls, shade 104 Natural White; E 3 [3, 3, 4, 4] x 25g (⁹/₁₀oz) balls, shade 577 Chestnut

Jamieson and Smith's 2-ply Jumper Weight (100% Shetland wool, approx 125 yards [115m])

C 2 [2, 2, 2, 2] x 25g (⁹/₁₀oz) balls, shade 4 (moorit brown); F 2 [2, 2, 2, 2] x 25g (⁹/₁₀oz) balls, shade 5 (Shetland black)

Needles

1 circular needle size 1 (2.75mm), 16 inches (40cm) long; 1 circular needle size 1 (2.75mm), 24 inches (60cm) long; 1 circular needle size 2 (3mm), 32 inches (80cm) long

Special abbreviation

m1 Pick up loop lying between sts and k tbl

❋ MEASUREMENTS

To fit chest 34 [36, 38, 40, 42] inches (86 [91, 97, 102, 107]cm)

Actual chest size 36¼ [38½, 41, 43, 45] inches (92 [98, 104, 109, 114]cm)

Length from back neck 21¾ [22¾, 22¾, 24, 24¾] inches (55 [58, 58, 61, 63]cm)

Gauge

33 sts and 38 rows measure 4 inches (10cm) over pattern on size 2 (3mm) needles (or size needed to obtain given gauge)

BACK AND FRONT

This garment is knitted in one piece to the armholes. Carry yarn not in use loosely across wrong side of work. Using smaller circular needle 24 inches (60cm) long and yarn A, cast on 284 [300, 316, 332, 348] sts. Cont in rounds as follows:

Rounds 1–4 (K2B, p2A) to end.
Rounds 5–8 (K2C, p2A) to end.
Rounds 9–12 (K2D, p2A) to end.
Rounds 13–16 (K2E, p2A) to end.
Rounds 17–24 As rounds 1–8.
Change to larger circular needle.
Next round **Using A, k6 [9, 7, 5, 10], *m1, k13 [12, 12, 12, 11]; rep from * 9 [10, 11, 12, 13] times, m1, k6 [9, 7, 5, 10]**; rep from ** to ** once. *306 [324, 342, 360, 378] sts.*
Cont in St st and patt as given on chart, reading rounds from right to left until work measures 13¾ [13¾, 13¾, 15, 15] inches (35 [35, 35, 38, 38]cm), finishing 10 [6, 11, 7, 12] sts before end of last round.

Divide for back and front

Next round *Bind off 20 [21, 22, 23, 24] sts, patt 133 [141, 149, 157, 165] sts including st used in binding off; rep from * once.
Complete back first. Cont in St st and patt from chart, reading p rows from left to right and working backward and forward as follows:
Next row Patt to end.
Next row K1, skpo, patt to last 3 sts, k2 tog, k1.
Rep last 2 rows until 97 [105, 111, 119, 125] sts rem. Cont straight until armholes measure 8 [9, 9, 9, 9¾] inches (20 [23, 23, 23, 25]cm), ending with a wrong-side row.

Shape shoulders

Next row Bind off 26 [30, 33, 37, 38] sts, patt to last 26 [30, 33, 37, 38] sts, bind off these sts. Leave rem 45 [45, 45, 45, 49] sts on a spare needle. With wrong side facing, rejoin appropriate yarn to rem sts.
Next row Patt 66 [70, 74, 78, 82] sts and turn

Key

A Prussian Blue
B Fool's Gold
C 4 (moorit brown)
D Natural White
E Chestnut
F 5 (Shetland black)

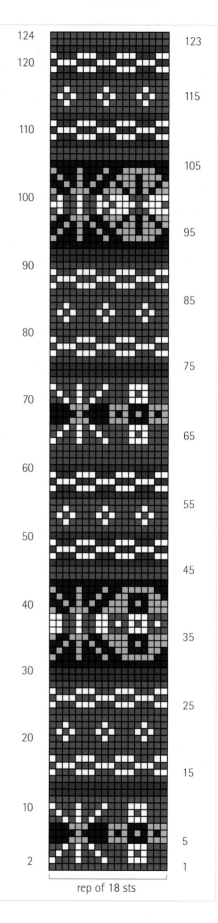

124 123
120
115
110
105
100
95
90
85
80
75
70
65
60
55
50
45
40
35
30
25
20
15
10
5
2   1

rep of 18 sts

leaving rem sts on a spare needle.
Complete right side of neck first.
Next row K2 tog, patt to last 3 sts, k2 tog, k1.
Next row Patt to end.
Rep last 2 rows 9 [5, 6, 6, 7] times.
Next row Patt to last 3 sts, k2 tog, k1.
Next row Patt to end.
Next row K2 tog, patt to last 3 sts, k2 tog. k1.
Next row Patt to end.
Rep last 4 rows 3 [5, 5, 5, 5] times. Keeping armhole edge straight, cont dec at neck edge until 26 [30, 33, 37, 38] sts rem. Cont straight until front matches back to shoulder, ending with a wrong-side row.
Bind off.
With wrong side of front facing, sl center st onto a safety pin, rejoin appropriate yarn to rem sts and patt to end.
Next row K1, skpo, patt to last 2 sts, k2 tog.
Next row Patt to end.
Rep last 2 rows 9 [5, 6, 6, 7] times.
Next row K1, skpo, patt to end.
Next row Patt to end.
Next row K1, skpo, patt to last 2 sts, k2 tog.
Next row Patt to end.
Complete as given for first side of neck.

NECKBAND

Join shoulder seams. With right side facing, using smaller circular needle 24 inches (60cm) long and yarn A, pick up and k 76 [84, 84, 84, 88] sts down left side neck, k center st on safety pin, pick up and k 76 [84, 84, 84, 88] sts up right side of neck, k across 45 [45, 45, 45, 49] center back sts inc 1 st at center. *199 [215, 215, 215, 227] sts.*
Work in rounds as follows:
Round 1 (K2E, p2A) 18 [20, 20, 20, 21] times, k2E, using A, skpo, k1, k2 tog, k2E, (p2A, k2E) 30 [32, 32, 32, 34] times.
Round 2 (K2E, p2A) 18 [20, 20, 20, 21] times, k1E, using E, skpo, k1A, using E, k2 tog, k1, (p2A, k2E) 30 [32, 32, 32, 34] times.
Round 3 (K2D, p2A) 18 [20, 20, 20, 21] times, using D, skpo, k1A, using D, k2 tog, (p2A, k2D) 30 [32, 32, 32, 34] times.
Round 4 (K2D, p2A) 17 [19, 19, 19, 20] times, k2D, using A, p1, yb, skpo, k1, k2 tog, p1, k2D, (p2A, k2D) 29 [31, 31, 31, 33] times.
Round 5 (K2C, p2A) 17 [19, 19, 19, 20] times, k2C, using A, skpo, k1, k2 tog, k2C, (p2A, k2C) 29 [31, 31, 31, 33] times.
Round 6 (K2C, p2A) 17 [19, 19, 19, 20] times, k1C, using C, skpo, k1A, using C, k2 tog, k1, (p2A, k2C) 29 [31, 31, 31, 33] times.
Round 7 (K2B, p2A) 17 [19, 19, 19, 20] times, using B, skpo, k1A, using B, k2 tog, (p2A, k2B) 29 [31, 31, 31, 33] times.
Round 8 (K2B, p2A) 16 [18, 18, 18, 19] times, k2B, using A, p1, yb, skpo, k1, k2 tog, p1, k2B, (p2A, k2B) 28 [30, 30, 30, 32] times.
Using A, bind off in rib, dec as before.

ARMBANDS

With right side facing, using smaller circular needle 16 inches (40cm) long, yarn A and beg at center of bound-off sts at armhole, pick up and k 156 [168, 168, 168, 184] sts evenly around armhole edge. Work in rounds as follows:
Rounds 1 and 2 (K2E, p2A) to end.
Rounds 3 and 4 (K2D, p2A) to end.
Rounds 5 and 6 (K2C, p2A) to end.
Rounds 7 and 8 (K2B, p2A) to end.
Using yarn A, bind off in rib.

FINISHING

Darn in any loose ends. Block as given on page 139.

OXO Fair Isle Crewneck

❋ MATERIALS

Yarns

Jamieson and Smith's 2-ply Jumper Weight (100% Shetland wool, approx 125 yards [115m]) A 6 [7, 7, 7] x 25g (⁹⁄₁₀oz) balls, shade 5 (Shetland black); B 2 [2, 3, 3] x 25g (⁹⁄₁₀oz) balls, shade 54 (dark gray); C 2 [2, 2, 2] x 25g (⁹⁄₁₀oz) balls, shade 27 (mid gray); D 7 [7, 7, 7] x 25g (⁹⁄₁₀oz) balls, shade 203 (light gray); E 3 [3, 3, 3] x 25g (⁹⁄₁₀oz) balls, shade 202 (fawn); F 4 [4, 4, 4] x 25g (⁹⁄₁₀oz) balls, shade 4 (moorit brown)

Needles

1 circular needle size 1 (2.75mm), 24 inches (60cm) long; 1 set of double-pointed needles size 1 (2.75mm); 1 circular needle size 2 (3mm), 32 inches (80cm) long; 1 circular needle size 2 (3mm), 16 inches (40cm) long

Notions

1 stitch holder

Special abbreviation

m1 Pick up loop lying between sts and k tbl

❋ MEASUREMENTS

To fit chest 34 [36, 38, 40] inches (86 [91, 97, 102]cm)
Actual chest size 37¾ [40½, 43, 45¼] inches (96 [103, 109, 115]cm)
Length from back neck 21¾ [22¾, 24¾, 25½] inches (55 [58, 63, 65]cm)
Sleeve seam 17 [17¾, 19¾, 19¾] inches (43 [45, 50, 50]cm)

Gauge

33 sts and 38 rows measure 4 inches (10cm) over pattern on size 2 (3mm) needles (or size needed to obtain given gauge)

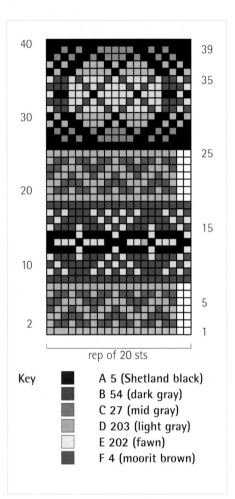

40
39
35
30
25
20
15
10
5
2
1

rep of 20 sts

Key
A 5 (Shetland black)
B 54 (dark gray)
C 27 (mid gray)
D 203 (light gray)
E 202 (fawn)
F 4 (moorit brown)

Note The small patterns (rows 1–7 and 19–25) do not always fall in the same place in relation to the larger motifs.

BACK AND FRONT

This garment is knitted in one piece to the armholes. Carry yarn not in use loosely across wrong side of work.

Using smaller circular needle and yarn A, cast on 280 [300, 320, 340] sts. Cont in rounds as follows:

Rounds 1–3 (K2B, p2A) to end.
Rounds 4–6 (K2C, p2A) to end.
Rounds 7 and 8 (K2D, p2A) to end.
Rounds 9 and 10 (K2E, p2A) to end.
Rounds 11 and 12 As rounds 7 and 8.
Rounds 13–15 As rounds 4 to 6.
Rounds 16–18 As rounds 1–3.

Change to larger circular needle 32 inches (80cm) long.

Next round Using A, *k7 [7, 8, 8], m1, k7 [8, 8, 9], m1; rep from * to end. *320 [340, 360, 380] sts.*

Reading rounds from right to left and beg with round 19 [8, 1, 1] cont in St st and patt from chart until work measures 13¾ [15, 15¾, 15¾] inches (35 [38, 40, 40]cm), ending with round 7 and 11 [7, 12, 8] sts before end of last round.

Divide for back and front

Next round *Bind off 23 [25, 25, 27], patt 137 [145, 155, 163] sts including st used in binding off; rep from * once.

Complete back first. Keeping continuity of patt, work backward and forward in St st, reading p rows from left to right from chart.

Next row (Wrong side) Patt to end.
Next row K1, skpo, patt to last 3 sts, k2 tog, k1.

Rep last 2 rows until 107 [113, 123, 129] sts rem. Cont straight until armholes measure 8 [8, 9, 9] inches (20 [20, 23, 23]cm), ending with a wrong-side row.

Shape shoulders

Next row Bind off 29 [31, 34, 36] sts, patt to last 29 [31, 34, 36] sts, bind off these sts.

Leave rem 49 [51, 55, 57] sts on a spare needle. With wrong side of front facing, rejoin appropriate yarn to rem sts.

Next row P1, p2 tog, patt to last 3 sts, p2 tog tbl, p1.
Next row K1, skpo, patt to last 3 sts, k2 tog, k1.

Rep last 2 rows 4 times.

Next row Patt to end.
Next row K1, skpo, patt to last 3 sts, k2 tog, k1.

Rep last 2 rows until 107 [113, 123, 129] sts rem. Cont straight until armholes measure 5 [5, 6, 6] inches (13 [13, 15, 15]cm), ending with a wrong-side row.

Shape neck

Next row Patt 36 [38, 42, 44] and turn; leave rem sts on needle. Complete left side first.
Next row Patt to end.
Next row Patt to last 2 sts, k2 tog.

Rep last 2 rows until 29 [31, 34, 36] sts rem. Cont straight until front matches back to shoulder, ending with a wrong-side row. Bind off. With right side of front facing, sl center

35 [37, 39, 41] sts onto stitch holder, rejoin appropriate yarn to rem sts and patt to end.
Next row Patt to end.
Next row Skpo, patt to end.
Complete as given for left side neck.
Join shoulder seams.

SLEEVES

With right side facing, using larger circular needle 16 inches (40cm) long, yarn A and beg at center of bound-off sts at armhole, pick up and k 140 [140, 160, 180] sts evenly around armhole edge. Cont in rounds of St st and patt from chart, working rounds in reverse order.
Rounds 1–7 As rounds 7–1.
Beg with round 40, cont in patt, work 15 [8, 15, 15] rounds.
Next round K1, k2 tog, patt to last 3 sts, skpo, k1.
Patt 5 [6, 6, 5] rounds straight. Keeping continuity of patt, rep last 6 [7, 7, 6] rounds until 100 [100, 120, 130] sts rem, ending with dec round. Patt 5 [0, 11, 0] rounds straight.
Next round Using A, k8 [8, 0, 2], (k2 tog, k1)

to last 8 [8, 0, 2] sts, k to end. *72 [72, 80, 88] sts.*
Change to double-pointed needles. Work 18 rounds in rib as given for waistband. Using A, bind off in rib.

NECKBAND

With right side facing, using double-pointed needles, pick up and k 22 [22, 25, 31] sts down left side neck, k across 35 [37, 39, 41] center front sts, pick up and k 22 [22, 25, 31] sts up right side neck and k across 49 [51, 55, 57] center back sts. *128 [132, 144, 160] sts.*
Round 1 (K2E, p2A) to end.
Rep this round 1 [1, 1, 2] times.
Next round (K2D, p2A) to end.
Rep last round 1 [1, 2, 2] times.
Next round (K2C, p2A) to end.
Rep last round 1 [2, 2, 2] times.
Next 3 rounds (K2B, p2A) to end.
Using A, bind off in rib.

FINISHING

Darn in loose ends. Block as given on page 139.

Aran

The Aran Islands lie off the west Atlantic coast of Ireland in the mouth of Galway bay—a position that has molded their lifestyle and culture. There are three main islands: Inishmore (meaning the big island), Inishmaan (the middle island) and Inisheer (the west island). The cliffs are steep and dangerous, the soil poor, and the sea can be rough; but in spite of this, the islanders for generations fished and farmed for a meager livelihood. The landscape features tiny fields divided by dry stone walls, where they raised cattle and sheep. Because of their isolation, the islanders had to be as self-sufficient as possible. They spun their wool into yarn, and wove and knitted their own warm garments.

This lifestyle was portrayed in the film *Man of Aran*, which was released in 1934 and romanticized the reality of the lives of the islanders. Although ostensibly a documentary, the film was highly scripted, blurring fact with fiction. In particular, it portrayed scenes of hunting a shark in a way that had not been done for several generations.

A similar confusion of fact and fiction arose concerning the origins of the Aran sweater. The first supposed Aran sweater was discovered by a German named Heinz Kiewe in a shop in Dublin in the 1930s. In 1967 he published his book *The Sacred History of Knitting*, in which he developed a theory—now thought to be based largely on his imagination— that similar sweaters had been knitted in Aran for generations and created a myth that the patterns were ancient Celtic ones. Kiewe had never even been to Aran, but his book was taken as gospel truth by many, and so the myth started to be believed as fact.

If we look at the oldest Aran sweaters, it seems more likely that these are related to the ganseys of the Scottish islands; perhaps a skilled knitter from Scotland brought her knowledge of stitch patterns to the Aran Island women. The knitting took on its distinctive local characteristics and became a cottage industry in the 1950s and 1960s, as it provided a source of income. By this time, the Aran sweater differed considerably from any original inspiration of Scottish ganseys. For one thing, the yarn was heavier, usually cream (natural white), and often oiled. The commercial consideration that this would knit up more quickly than fine wool probably had some influence here. Aran garments are now knitted in separate pieces, rather than in the round, but both methods were used by the earlier knitters, as can be seen in the garments displayed in the National Museum in Dublin. Some garments in this museum feature fancy openwork patterns, which reinforces the idea that they are related to the openwork ganseys of the Western Isles of Scotland.

The Aran knitting that has become so popular today has a strong identity of its own, with features that distinguish it from other types of knitting. Perhaps the most important of these is the fact that nearly all the cables, diagonals making trellis or lattice patterns, and other patterns are composed of knit stitches traveling across a purl-stitch background. This has the result of raising the pattern into a texture of considerable depth; the use of bobbles enhances this embossed texture. The gansey, on the other hand, uses the opposite effect, having patterns raised on a plain stockinette-stitch background.

Another difference between ganseys and Aran knits is that the stitch patterns in Aran nearly always run vertically, with no division between the body and yoke of the garment. Also, the sleeves are usually set in and the whole garment seamed. However, the two styles share many stitch patterns and motifs, such as Tree of Life and diamond, or lozenge, patterns. Cables, too, are common to both styles, but in Aran the cable is exploited to create many variations; for example, it can be divided into a lattice pattern or split to form a chevron.

Whether old or new, Aran knitting has now become part of the folk craft of Ireland and is today one of the most distinctive and recognizable knitting styles. The garments in this book show some of these stitches used in different weights of yarn and in different shapes, but all relate to what we know as the familiar Aran style of knitting.

Cable and Moss Aran Tunic

A contemporary design featuring traditional stitch patterns—medallion cable and moss stitch—this long, loose-fitting sweater is roomy enough to be worn over several layers of clothing and can replace a jacket on spring or autumn days in the country.

Chevron Aran Crewneck

Classic Aran stitches—crossover chevron and Irish moss stitch—are used on this roomy dropped-shoulder pullover. Shown here in the traditional natural white, it would look just as effective in the shade of your choice. The pattern is sized to suit both women and men.

Tree of Life Aran Jacket

Two famous Aran patterns, the Tree of Life and chain cable, are worked into this woman's jacket. The Tree of Life is an ancient religious symbol, which is also said to represent family connections; the chain cable is related to the honeycomb pattern, a very old traditional pattern.

Wheat Cable Cotton Sweater

A delicate wheat cable pattern used in two different combinations decorates this versatile cotton shirt-style sweater for relaxing in the country or wearing in town. Elaborate, patterned waistbands and cuffs are interesting characteristics peculiar to Aran knitting.

Fountain Lace Short-Sleeve Sweater

The bold patterns of Aran are transformed in a fine cotton yarn to make this delicate sweater combining bands of fountain lace and plaited cable. A neat collar and buttons at the back of the neck complete a classic, summery cotton top.

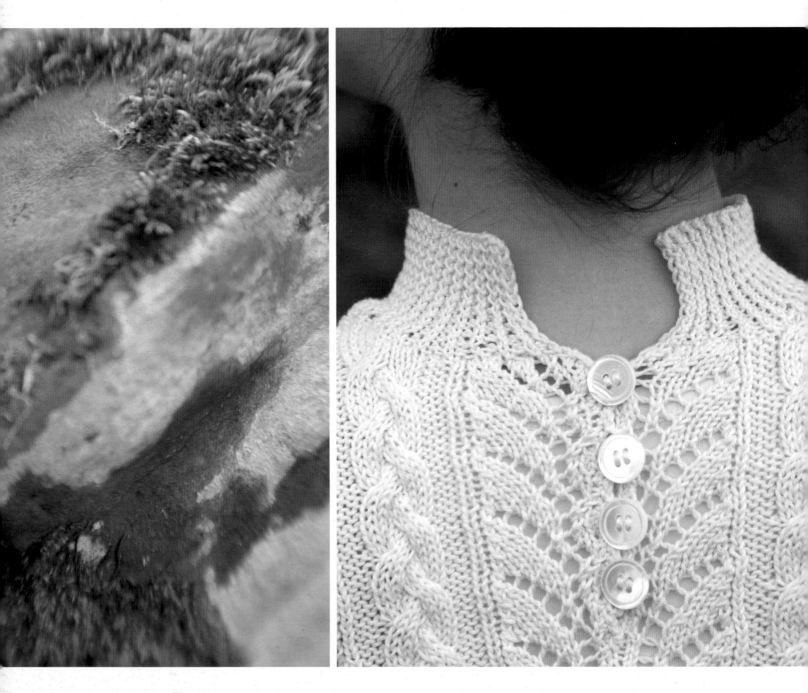

Classic Cotton Crewneck

This traditional crewneck sweater features a variety of stitch patterns, including a central honeycomb panel, Aran diamonds with moss stitch, and knotted chain cable. Either double-knitting-weight cotton, as here, or the same weight in wool can be used.

Cable and Moss Aran Tunic

❊ **MATERIALS**

Yarn

10 [11, 12] x 100g (3½oz) balls Rowan
Pure Wool Aran (approx 186 yards
[170m]), shade 674 Cedar

Needles

1 pair size 7 (4.5mm); 1 pair size 8
(5mm); 1 cable needle

Special abbreviations

c4f Sl next 2 sts onto cable needle and
leave at front of work, k2 from left-hand
needle, k2 from cable needle

c4b Sl next 2 sts onto cable needle and
leave at back of work, k2 from left-hand
needle, k2 from cable needle

❊ **MEASUREMENTS**

To fit chest 36 [38, 40] inches
(91 [96, 102]cm)

Actual chest size 41¾ [43¼, 45¾] inches
(106 [110, 116]cm)

Length from back neck 26 [27¼, 28¼]
inches (66 [69, 72]cm)

Sleeve seam 18 inches (45cm)

Gauge

22 sts and 26 rows measure 4 inches
(10cm) over pattern on size 8 (5mm)
needles (or size needed to obtain
given gauge)

CABLE PANEL

Repeat of 13 sts.

Row 1 (Right side) P2, k9, p2.

Row 2 K2, p9, k2.

Rows 3 and 4 As rows 1 and 2.

Row 5 P2, c4f, k1, c4b, p2.

Row 6 As row 2.

Rows 7–12 Rep rows 1 and 2, 3 times.

Row 13 As row 5.

Row 14 As row 2.

Rows 15–20 Rep rows 1 and 2, 3 times.

Row 21 P2, c4b, k1, c4f, p2.

Row 22 As row 2.

Rows 23–26 Rep rows 1
and 2 twice.

These 26 rows form cable panel.

BACK

Using smaller needles, cast
on 119 [123, 131] sts.

Row 1 (Right side) K1,
(p1, k1) to end.

Row 2 P1, (k1, p1)
to end.

Rep these two rows until rib
measures 2 inches (5cm), ending
with a row 1. Purl 1 row. Change
to larger needles. Begin patt.

Row 1 K1, (p1, k1) 8 [9, 11] times,
*work next 13 sts as row 1 of cable
panel, k1, (p2, k1) 5 times; rep from
* 3 times, (p1, k1) 3 [4, 6] times.

Row 2 P1, (k1, p1) 8 [9, 11] times,
*work next 13 sts as row 2 of cable
panel, p1, (k1, p1) 5 times; rep from
* 3 times, (k1, p1) 3 [4, 6] times.

Row 3 P1, (k1, p1) 8 [9, 11] times, *work
next 13 sts as row 3 of cable panel, p1,
(k1, p1) 5 times; rep from * 3 times, (k1, p1)
3 [4, 6] times.

Row 4 K1, (p1, k1) 8 [9, 11] times, *work
next 13 sts as row 4 of cable panel, k1,
(p1, k1) 5 times; rep from * 3 times, (p1, k1)
3 [4, 6] times.

These 4 rows establish moss st patt.

Cont in patt as set, working appropriate rows
of cable panel until work measures 25¼ [26½,
27½] inches (64 [67, 70]cm), ending with a
right-side row.

Shape neck

Next row Patt 42 [43, 46], bind off next 35
[37, 39] sts, patt to end.

Complete right side of back neck first. Dec
1 st at neck edge on every row until 37
[38, 41] sts rem. Patt 1 row. Bind off. With
right side facing, rejoin yarn to rem sts, k2
tog, patt to end. Complete to match first
side of neck.

POCKET LININGS

Using larger needles, cast on 31 sts. Beg with
a k row, work 6 inches (15cm) in St st, ending
with a p row. Leave these sts on a spare needle.
Make another pocket lining to match.

FRONT

Work as given for back until work measures
8 inches (20cm), ending with a wrong-side row.

Place pockets

Next row Patt 10 [12, 16], sl next 31 sts onto
a stitch holder, patt across 31 sts of first
pocket lining, patt 37, sl next 31 sts onto a
stitch holder, patt across 31 sts of second
pocket lining, patt to end.

Cont in patt until front measures 23¼ [24½,
25½] inches (59 [62, 65]cm), ending with a
right-side row.

Shape neck

Next row Patt 46 [47, 50], bind off next 27
[29, 31] sts, patt to end.

Complete left side of neck first. Dec 1 st at neck edge on every row until 37 [38, 41] sts rem. Cont straight until front matches back to shoulder, ending with a wrong-side row. Bind off. With right side facing, rejoin yarn to rem sts, k2 tog, patt to end. Complete to match first side of neck.

SLEEVES

Using smaller needles, cast on 59 sts. Work 2 inches (5cm) in rib as given for back waistband, ending with a first row.
Next row P2, (inc in next st, p4) to last 2 sts, inc in next st, p1. *71 sts.*
Change to larger needles. Begin patt.
Row 1 K1, (p1, k1) twice, *work next 13 sts as row 1 of cable panel, k1, (p1, k1) 5 times; rep from * once, work next 13 sts as row 1 of cable panel, k1, (p1, k1) twice.
Row 2 P1, (k1, p1) twice, *work next 13 sts as row 2 of cable panel, p1, (k1, p1) 5 times; rep from * once, work next 13 sts as row 2 of cable panel, p1, (k1, p1) twice.

Row 3 P1, (k1, p1) twice, *work next 13 sts as row 3 of cable panel, p1, (k1, p1) 5 times; rep from * once, work next 13 sts as row 3 of cable panel, p1, (k1, p1) twice.
Row 4 K1, (p1, k1) twice, *work next 13 sts as row 4 of cable panel, k1, (p1, k1) 5 times; rep from * once, work next 13 sts as row 4 of cable panel, k1, (p1, k1) twice.
These 4 rows establish moss st patt.
Cont in patt as set, working appropriate rows of cable panel. Inc 1 st at each end of next row and 8 foll 3rd rows, then on every foll 4th row until there are 117 sts, working extra sts into moss st patt. Cont straight until sleeve measures 17¼ inches (44cm), ending with a wrong-side row. Beg with a p row, work 2 rows St st. Bind off.

NECKBAND

With right side facing, join right shoulder seam. With right side facing and using smaller needles, pick up and k 20 sts down left side of front neck, 25 [27, 29] sts from center front,

20 sts up right side of front neck, 6 sts down right side of back neck, 32 [34, 36] sts from center back and 63 sts up left side of back neck. *109 [113, 117] sts.*
Beg with a row 2, work 12 rows in rib as for back waistband. Bind off in rib.

POCKET EDGINGS

With right side facing and using smaller needles, rejoin yarn to the 31 sts left on holder. Beg with a row 1, work 6 rows in rib as given for back waistband. Bind off in rib.

FINISHING

Block each piece as given on page 139. With right sides facing, join left shoulder seam. Fold neckband in half to wrong side and slipstitch. Catch down pocket linings and sides of pocket edgings. Mark position of armholes 10¼ inches (26cm) down from shoulders on back and front. Sew in sleeves between markers. Join side and sleeve seams.

Chevron Aran Crewneck

❋ MATERIALS

Yarn

9 [9, 10] x 100g (3½oz) balls Rowan Pure
Wool Aran (approx 170m [186 yards]),
shade 670 Ivory

Needles

1 pair size 6 (4mm)
1 pair size 8 (5mm)
1 cable needle

Special abbreviations

cr5 Sl next 3 sts onto cable needle and
leave at back of work, k2 from left-hand
needle, then p1, k2 from cable needle
cr3r Sl next st onto cable needle and leave
at back of work, k2 from left-hand needle,
p1 from cable needle

cr3l Sl next 2 sts onto cable needle and
leave at front of work, p1 from left-
hand needle, k2 from cable needle

❋ MEASUREMENTS

To fit chest 36 [38, 40] inches
(91 [97, 102]cm)
Actual chest size 44 [45¾, 48¾] inches
(112 [116, 124]cm)
Length to shoulder 26 [27¼, 28¼] inches
(66 [69, 72]cm)
Sleeve seam 17¼ inches (44cm)

Gauge

21 sts and 23 rows measure 4 inches (10cm)
over pattern on size 8 (5mm) needles (or
size needed to obtain given gauge)

PATTERN PANEL

Worked over 19 sts.

Row 1 (Right side) K1 tbl, p6, k2, p1, k2, p6, k1 tbl.
Row 2 P1, k6, p2, k1, p2, k6, p1.
Row 3 K1 tbl, p6, cr5, p6, k1 tbl.
Row 4 As row 2.
Row 5 K1 tbl, p5, cr3r, k1, cr3l, p5, k1 tbl.
Row 6 P1, k5, p2, k1, p1, k1, p2, k5, p1.
Row 7 K1 tbl, p4, cr3r, k1, p1, k1, cr3l, p4, k1 tbl.
Row 8 P1, k4, p2, (k1, p1) twice, k1, p2, k4, p1.
Row 9 K1 tbl, p3, cr3r, (k1, p1) twice, k1, cr3l, p3, k1 tbl.
Row 10 P1, k3, p2, (p1, k1) 3 times, k1, p2, k3, p1.
Row 11 K1 tbl, p2, cr3r, (k1, p1) 3 times, k1, cr3l, p2, k1 tbl.
Row 12 P1, k2, p2, (k1, p1) 4 times, k1, p2, k2, p1.
Row 13 K1 tbl, p1, cr3r, (k1, p1) 4 times, k1, cr3l, p1, k1 tbl.
Row 14 P1, k1, p2, (k1, p1) 5 times, k1, p2, k1, p1.
Row 15 K1 tbl, p1, k2, p3, k2, p1, k2, p3, k2, p1, k1 tbl.
Rows 2–15 form panel pattern.

BACK

Using smaller needles, cast on 110 [114, 118] sts.

Row 1 (Right side) K2, (p2, k2) to end.
Row 2 P2, (k2, p2) to end.
Rep these 2 rows until rib measures 4 inches
(10cm), ending with row 1.
Next row Rib 5 [7, 3], *inc in next st, rib 9 [9,
7]; rep from * to last 5 [7, 3] sts, inc in next st,
rib to end. *121 [125, 133] sts.*
Change to larger needles. Begin patt.
Row 1 K1, (p1, k1) 5 [6, 8] times, *p2, work
row 1 of panel patt, p2, k1, (p1, k1) 7 times;
rep from * once, p2, work row 1 of panel
patt, p2, (k1, p1) 5 [6, 8] times, k1.
Row 2 P1, (k1, p1) 5 [6, 8] times, *k2, work
row 2 of panel patt, k2, p1, (k1, p1) 7 times;
rep from * once, k2, work row 2 of panel patt,
k2, (p1, k1) 5 [6, 8] times, p1.
Row 3 P1, (k1, p1) 5 [6, 8] times, *p2, work
3rd row of panel patt, p3, (k1, p1) 7 times; rep
from * once, p2, work row 3 of panel patt, p2,
(p1, k1) 5 [6, 8] times, p1.
Row 4 K1, (p1, k1) 5 [6, 8] times, *k2, work
row 4 of panel patt, k3, (p1, k1) 7 times; rep
from * once, k2, work row 4 of panel patt, k2,
(k1, p1) 5 [6, 8] times, k1.
These 4 rows establish moss st patt. Cont in
patt as set, working appropriate rows of panel
patt until work measures 24¾ [26, 27¼] inches

(63 [66, 69]cm), ending with a wrong-side row.
Shape neck
Next row Patt 49 [51, 53] sts and turn; leave
rem sts on a spare needle. Complete right side
of neck first. Dec 1 st at neck edge on next 5
rows. *44 [46, 48] sts.*
Patt 2 rows. Bind off.
With right side facing, sl center 23 [23, 27] sts
onto a holder, rejoin yarn to rem sts and patt
to end. Complete to match first side of neck.

FRONT

Work as given for back until work measures
22¾ [24, 25¼] inches (58 [61, 64]cm), ending
with a wrong-side row.
Shape neck
Next row Patt 49 [51, 53] sts and turn; leave
rem sts on a spare needle. Complete left side
of neck first.
Dec 1 st at neck edge on next 5 rows. *44 [46,
48] sts.* Cont straight until front matches back
to shoulder, ending with a wrong-side row.

Bind off.

With right side facing, sl center 23 [23, 27] sts onto holder, rejoin yarn to rem sts and patt to end. Complete to match first side of neck.

SLEEVES

Using smaller needles, cast on 54 sts. Work 4 inches (10cm) in rib as given for back waistband, ending with a row 1.

Next row Rib 3 (inc in next st, rib 2) to end. *71 sts.*

Change to larger needles. Begin patt.

Row 1 K1, (p1, k1) twice, p2, work row 1 of panel patt, p2, k1, (p1, k1) 7 times, p2, work row 1 of panel patt, p2, (k1, p1) twice, k1.

Row 2 P1, (k1, p1) twice, k2, work row 2 of panel patt, k2, p1, (k1, p1) 7 times, k2, work row 2 of panel patt, k2, (p1, k1) twice, p1.

Row 3 P1, (k1, p1) twice, p2, work row 3 of panel patt, p3, (k1, p1) 7 times, p2, work row 3 of panel patt, p2, (p1, k1) twice, p1.

Row 4 K1, (p1, k1) twice, k2, work row 4 of panel patt, k3, (p1, k1) 7 times, k2, work row 4 of panel patt, k2, (k1, p1) twice, k1.

These 4 rows establish moss st patt. Cont in patt as set, working appropriate rows of panel patt, inc 1 st at each end of next row and every foll row 4 until there are 109 sts, working extra sts into moss st patt. Patt 1 row. Work should measure 17 inches (43cm). Purl 1 row. Knit 1 row. Bind off.

NECKBAND

Join right shoulder seam. With right side facing and using smaller needles, pick up and k 20 sts down left side of front neck, k 23 [23, 27] center front sts, pick up and k 20 sts up right side of front neck, 8 sts down right side of back neck, k 23 [23, 27] center back sts, pick up and k 8 sts up left side of back neck. *102 [102, 110] sts.*

Beg with a row 2, work 15 rows in rib as given for back waistband. Bind off in rib.

FINISHING

Block each piece as given on page 139. Join left shoulder and neckband seam. Fold neckband in half to wrong side and slipstitch in place. Mark positions of armholes 9¾ inches (25cm) down from shoulders on back and front. Sew in sleeves. Join side and sleeve seams.

Tree of Life Aran Jacket

❖ MATERIALS

Yarn
10 [10, 10, 11] x 100g (3½oz) balls Rowan Pure Wool Aran (approx 186 yards [170m]), shade 675 Sage

Needles
1 pair size 5 (3.75mm)
1 pair size 7 (4.5mm)
1 cable needle

Notions
3 buttons, 2 inches (2.5cm) in diameter
3 stitch holders

Special abbreviations
c4f Sl next 2 sts onto cable needle and leave at front of work, k2 from left-hand needle, k2 from cable needle
c4b Sl next 2 sts onto cable needle and leave at back of work, k2 from left-hand needle, k2 from cable needle
cr2r Sl next st onto cable needle and leave at back of work, k1, p1 from cable needle
cr2l Sl next st onto cable needle and leave at front of work, p1, k1 from cable needle
tw2 K into front of 2nd st then k first 2, sl both sts off needle tog

❖ MEASUREMENTS
To fit chest 32-34 [36-38, 40-42, 44-46] inches (81-86 [91-96, 102-107, 112-116]cm)
Actual chest size 41¼ [45, 49½, 54¼] inches (105 [114, 126, 138]cm)
Length from back neck 25½ [26, 26¼, 26¾] inches (65 [66, 67, 68]cm)
Sleeve seam 16½ [17, 17, 17¼] inches (42 [43, 43, 44]cm)

Gauge
20 sts and 26 rows measure 4 inches (10cm) over pattern on size 7 (4.5mm) needles (or size needed to obtain given gauge)

CABLE PANEL

Repeat of 8 sts.
Row 1 (Wrong side) P8.
Row 2 C4b, c4f.
Row 3 P8.
Row 4 K8.
Row 5 P8.
Row 6 C4f, c4b.
Rows 7 and 8 As rows 3 and 4.
These 8 rows form cable panel.

TREE OF LIFE PANEL

Repeat of 12 sts.
Row 1 (Wrong side) K4, p4, k4.
Row 2 P3, cr2r, tw2, cr2l, p3.
Row 3 K3, (p1, k1, p1) twice, k3.
Row 4 P2, cr2r, p1, tw2, p1, cr2l, p2.
Row 5 K2, (p1, k2, p1) twice, k2.
Row 6 P1, cr2r, p2, tw2, p2, cr2l, p1.
Row 7 K1, (p1, k3, p1) twice, k1.
Row 8 Cr2r, p3, tw2, p3, cr2l.
These 8 rows form Tree of Life panel.

POCKET LININGS

Using larger needles, cast on 24 sts. Work 4¾ inches (12cm) in St st, ending with a p row.
Next row (K1, inc in next st, k1) to end. *32 sts.*
Leave these sts on a spare needle. Make another pocket lining to match.

BREAST POCKET LINING

Using larger needles, cast on 16 sts. Work 3¼ inches (8cm) in St st, ending with a p row.
Next row (K2, inc in next st, k1) to end. *20 sts.*
Leave these sts on a spare needle.

LEFT FRONT

Using smaller needles, cast on 41 [45, 50, 56] sts.
Row 1 (Right side) K1 [1, 0, 0] tbl, (p1, k1 tbl) to end.
Row 2 (P1, k1 tbl) to last 1 [1, 0, 0] sts, p1 [1, 0, 0].
Rep these two rows once.
1st and 2nd sizes
***Next row** (Rib 1, inc in next st) 3 times, *rib 4 [5], inc in next st, rib 2, inc in next st, rib 4 [5], inc in next st, (rib 1, inc in next st) twice; rep from * once, rib 1. *54 [58] sts.*
Change to larger needles. Begin patt.
Row 1 (Wrong side) K1, *work row 1 of cable panel, k1 [2], work row 1 of Tree of Life panel, k1 [2]; rep from * once, work row 1 of cable panel, k1.
Row 2 P1, work row 2 of cable panel, *p1 [2], work row 2 of Tree of Life panel, p1 [2], work

row 2 of cable panel; rep from * once, p1***.

3rd and 4th sizes

Next row (Rib 1, inc in next st) 3 times, *rib [4, 5], inc in next st, rib 2, inc in next st, rib [4, 5], inc in next st, (rib 1, inc in next st) twice; rep from * once, rib [3, 4], inc in next st, rib 2, inc in next st, rib [3, 4]. *[65, 71] sts.*

Change to larger needles. Begin patt.

Row 1 (Wrong side) K [0, 1], work row 1 of Tree of Life panel, k [0, 1], *work row 1 of cable panel, k [1, 2], work row 1 of Tree of Life panel, k [1, 2]; rep from * once, work row 1 of cable panel, k1.

Row 2 P1, work row 2 of cable panel, *p [1, 2], work row 2 of Tree of Life panel, p [1, 2], work row 2 of cable panel; rep from * once, p [0, 1], work row 2 of Tree of Life panel, p [0, 1].

All sizes

These 2 rows establish patt. Cont in patt as set, working appropriate rows of panels, patt 11 rows.

Dec row Patt 9, p2 tog, patt to end. Patt 11 rows straight.

Dec row Patt 20 [22, 20, 22], p2 tog, patt to end. Patt 5 rows straight.

Place pocket

Next row Patt 11 [14, 19, 23] sts, sl next 32 sts onto a stitch holder, patt across 32 sts of pocket lining, patt to end.
Patt 5 rows straight.

Dec row Patt 29 [31, 29, 31], p2 tog, patt to end. Patt 11 rows straight.

Dec row Patt 40 [44, 40, 44], p2 tog, patt to end. *50 [54, 61, 67] sts.*
Patt 5 rows straight.

Shape front

Dec 1 st at end of next row of 6 foll 8th rows. Patt 1 row. Work should measure 16½ inches (42cm) from beg.

Shape armholes

Bind off 9 sts at beg of next row. Patt 1 row.

Place breast pocket

Next row Work 2 tog, patt 5 [7, 11, 14] , sl next 20 sts onto a stitch holder, patt across breast pocket lining, patt to end. Cont dec 1 st at front edge on foll row 4 and 2 [2, 4, 5] foll 8th rows and at the same time dec 1 st at armhole edge on foll 7 [11, 10, 12] alt rows. *23 [23, 29, 32] sts.*

Cont straight until armhole measures 8¼ [8¾,

9, 9½] inches (21 [22, 23, 24]cm), ending at armhole edge.

Shape shoulder

Bind off 8 [8, 10, 11] sts at beg of next row and foll alt row. Patt 1 row. Bind off rem 7 [7, 9, 10] sts.

RIGHT FRONT

Using smaller needles, cast on 41 [45, 50, 56] sts. Work 4 rows in rib as given for left front waistband.

1st and 2nd sizes

Work as given for left front from *** to ***.

3rd and 4th sizes

Next row Rib [3, 4], inc in next st, rib 2, inc in next st, rib [3, 4], inc in next st, (rib 1, inc in next st) twice, *rib [4, 5], inc in next st, rib 2, inc in next st, rib [4, 5], inc in next st, (rib 1, inc in next st) twice; rep from * once, rib 1. *[65, 71] sts.*

Change to larger needles. Begin patt.

Row 1 (Wrong side) K1, work row 1 of cable panel, *k [1, 2], work row 1 of Tree of Life panel, k [1, 2], work row 1 of cable panel; rep from * once, k [0, 1], work row 1 of Tree of Life panel, k [0, 1].

Row 2 P [0, 1], work row 2 of Tree of Life panel, p [0, 1], work row 2 of cable panel, *p [1, 2], work row 2 of Tree of Life panel, p [1, 2], work row 2 of cable panel; rep from * once, p1.

All sizes

These 2 rows establish patt. Cont in patt as set, working appropriate rows of panels, patt 11 rows.

Dec row Patt to last 11 sts, p2 tog tbl, patt to end. Patt 11 rows straight.

Dec row Patt to last 22 [24, 22, 24] sts, p2 tog tbl, patt to end.
Patt 5 rows straight.

Place pocket

Next row Patt 9 [10, 12, 14], sl next 32 sts onto a stitch holder, patt across 32 sts of pocket lining, patt to end.
Patt 5 rows straight.

Dec row Patt to last 31 [33, 31, 33] sts, p2 tog tbl, patt to end.
Patt 11 rows straight.

Dec row Patt to last 42 [46, 42, 46] sts, p2 tog tbl, patt to end. *50 [54, 61, 67] sts.*

Patt 5 rows straight.

Shape front

Dec 1 st at beg of next row and 6 foll 8th rows. Patt 2 rows.

Shape armhole Bind off 9 sts at beg of next row.

Next row Patt to last 2 sts, work 2tog.
Complete as given for left front.

BACK

Using smaller needles, cast on 90 [100, 105, 117] sts. Work 4 rows in rib as given for 3rd [3rd, first, first] sizes on left front waistband.

Next row (Rib 1, inc in next st) 3 times, *rib 4 [5, 4, 5], inc in next st, rib 2, inc in next st, rib 4 [5, 4, 5], inc in next st, (rib 1, inc in next st) twice*; rep from * to * once, **rib 3 [4, 3, 4], inc in next st, rib 2, inc in next st, rib 3 [4, 3, 4], inc in next st, (rib 1, inc in next st) twice **; rep from ** to ** 0 [0, 1, 1,] time, now rep from * to * twice, rib 1. *118 [128, 138, 150] sts.*

Change to larger needles. Begin patt.

Row 1 (Wrong side) K1, work row 1 of cable panel, *k1 [2, 1, 2], work row 1 of Tree of Life panel, k1 [2, 1, 2], work row 1 of cable panel*; rep from * to * once, **k0 [1, 0, 1], work row 1 of Tree of Life panel, k0 [1, 0, 1], work row 1 of cable panel**; rep from ** to ** 0 [0, 1, 1,] time, rep from * to * twice, k1.

Row 2 P1, work row 2 of cable panel, *p1 [2, 1, 2], work row 2 of Tree of Life panel, p1 [2, 1, 2], work row 2 of cable panel*; rep from * to * once, **p0 [1, 0, 1], work row 2 of Tree of Life panel, p0 [1, 0, 1], work row 2 of cable panel**; rep from ** to ** 0 [0, 1, 1] time, now rep from * to * twice, p1. These 2 rows establish patt. Cont in patt as set, working appropriate rows of panels, patt 11 rows.

Dec row Patt 9, p2 tog, patt to last 11 sts, p2 tog tbl, patt to end.
Patt 11 rows straight.

Dec row Patt 20 [22, 20, 22], p2 tog, patt to last 22 [24, 22, 24] sts, p2 tog tbl, patt to end.
Patt 11 rows straight.

Dec row Patt 29 [31, 29, 31], p2 tog, patt to last 31 [33, 31, 33] sts, p2 tog tbl, patt to end.
Patt 11 rows straight.

Dec row Patt 40 [44, 40, 44], p2 tog, patt to last 42 [46, 42, 46] sts, p2 tog tbl, patt to end. *110 [120, 130, 142] sts.*

Cont straight in patt until back matches front to armhole shaping, ending with a wrong-side row.

Shape armholes
Bind off 9 sts at beg of next 2 rows. Dec 1 st at each end of next row and every foll alt row until 74 [78, 90, 98] sts rem. Cont straight until back matches front to shoulder ending with a wrong-side row.

Shape shoulders
Bind off 8 [8, 10, 11] sts at beg of next 4 rows and 7 [7, 9, 10] sts at beg of foll 2 rows. Bind off rem 28 [32, 32, 34] sts.

SLEEVES

Using smaller needles, cast on 49 sts. Work 4 rows in rib as given for first size on left front waistband.
Next row Rib 7, *(inc in next st, rib 1) 3 times, (rib 2, inc in next st) twice, rib 3; rep from * once, (inc in next st, rib 1) 3 times, rib 6. *62 sts.* Change to larger needles. Begin patt.

Row 1 (Wrong side) P3, k4, (work row 1 of cable panel then row 1 of Tree of Life panel) twice, work row 1 of cable panel, k4, p3.
Row 2 Tw2, cr2l, p3, (work row 2 of cable panel then row 2 of Tree of Life panel) twice, work row 2 of cable panel, p3, cr3r, tw2. These 2 rows establish patt. Cont in patt as set, working appropriate rows of panels and inc 1 st at each end of 3rd row and every foll 7th [6th, 5th, 5th] row until there are 86 [90, 94, 96] sts, working extra sts into patt. Cont straight until sleeve measures 16½ [17, 17, 17¼] inches (42 [43, 43, 44]cm), ending with a wrong-side row.
Shape top Bind off 9 sts at beg of next 2 rows. Dec 1 st at each end of next row and every foll alt row until 50 sts rem, then on every row until 16 sts rem. Bind off.

BUTTON BANDS AND COLLAR

Button band and collar
Join shoulder seams. Using smaller needles,

cast on 11 sts. Work in rib as given for first size on left front until band when slightly stretched fits along left front to front shaping, ending with a wrong-side row.

Shape collar
Cont in rib, inc 1 st at beg of next row and every foll alt row until there are 28 sts then on every foll 4th row until there are 34 [34, 36, 36] sts. Cont straight until collar fits along shaped edge of front to center back neck. Bind off in rib. Sew in place.

Buttonhole band and collar
Mark button band with pins to indicate buttons, first one to come ¾ inches (2cm) up from cast on edge and last one 1¼ inches (3cm) below beg of collar shaping, rem one spaced equally between. Work as given for button band, reversing collar shaping and working buttonholes at pin positions as follows:
Buttonhole row Rib 5, bind off 2, rib to end.
Next row Rib to end, casting on 2 sts over those bound off in previous row.
Sew in place then join back seam of collar.

POCKET EDGINGS

With right side facing and using smaller needles, rejoin yarn to the 32 sts left on stitch holder.
Next row K1 tbl, p1, (k1 tbl, p1, k1 tbl, p2 tog) 5 times, (k1 tbl, p1) twice, k1 tbl. *27 sts.*
Beg with a row 2, work 7 rows in rib as given for first size on left front waistband. Bind off in rib.

Breast pocket edging
With right side facing and using smaller needles, rejoin yarn to the 20 sts left on stitch holder.
Next row K1 tbl, p1, (k1 tbl, p1, k1 tbl, p2 tog) 3 times, k1 tbl, p1, k1 tbl. *17 sts.*
Beg with a row 2, work 3 rows in rib as given for first size on left front waistband. Bind off in rib.

FINISHING

Block each piece as given on page 139. Catch down pocket linings and sides of pocket edgings. Join side and sleeve seams. Sew in sleeves. Sew on buttons.

Wheat Cable Cotton Sweater

❋ MATERIALS

Yarn

5 [5, 6, 6] x 100g (3½oz) balls Patons 100% mercerized cotton 4-ply (361 yards [330m]), shade 1716 Limestone

Needles

1 pair size 2 (2.75mm)

1 pair size 3 (3.25mm)

1 cable needle

Notions

4 buttons ⅜ inches (1cm) in diameter

Special abbreviations

c4f Sl next 2 sts onto cable needle and leave at front of work, k2 from left-hand needle, k2 from cable needle

c4b Sl next 2 sts onto cable needle and leave at back of work, k2 from left-hand needle, k2 from cable needle

cr3r Sl next st onto cable needle and leave at back of work, k2 from left-hand needle, p1 from cable needle

cr3l Sl next 2 sts onto cable needle and leave at front of work, p1 from left-hand needle, k2 from cable needle

❋ MEASUREMENTS

To fit chest 32 [34, 36, 38] inches (81 [86, 91, 97]cm)

Actual chest size 36¼ [37¾, 40¼, 41¾] inches (92 [96, 102, 106]cm)

Length to back neck 24 [24, 24½, 24½] inches (61 [61, 62, 62]cm)

Sleeve seam 17¼ [17¾, 18, 18½] inches (44 [45, 46, 47]cm)

Gauge

32 sts and 36 rows measure 4 inches (10cm) over pattern on size 3 (3.25mm) needles (or size needed to obtain given gauge)

BACK

Using smaller needles, cast on 119 [125, 132, 138] sts.

Row 1 (Wrong side) K2 [1, 2, 1], (p1, k1) 4 [6, 4, 6] times, *p8, k1 (p1, k1) twice; rep from * to last 5 [8, 5, 8] sts, (p1, k1) 2 [4, 2, 4] times, k1 [0, 1, 0].

Row 2 K0 [1, 0, 1], (k1, p1) 5 [6, 5, 6] times, *c4f, c4b, p1, (k1, p1) twice; rep from * to last 5 [8, 5, 8] sts, (k1, p1) 2 [3, 2, 3] times, k1 [2, 1, 2].

Row 3 As row 1.

Row 4 K0 [1, 0, 1], (k1, p1) 5 [6, 5, 6] times, *k8, p1, (k1, p1) twice; rep from * to last 5 [8, 5, 8] sts, (k1, p1) 2 [3, 2, 3] times, k1 [2, 1, 2]. Rep these 4 rows 7 times, then work rows 1 to 3 once.

Next row K0 [1, 0, 1], (inc in next st, p1) 5 [6, 5, 6] times, *k8, inc in next st, (k1, inc in next st) twice; rep from * to last 18 [21, 18, 21] sts, k8, (p1, inc in next st) 5 [6, 5, 6] times, k0 [1, 0, 1]. *150 [158, 166, 174] sts.*

Change to larger needles. Begin patt.

Row 1 K15 [19, 15, 19], (p8, k8) to last 7 [11, 7, 11] sts, k7 [11, 7, 11].

Row 2 P15 [19, 15, 19], (c4f, c4b, p8) to last 7 [11, 7, 11] sts, p7 [11, 7, 11].

Row 3 As row 1.

Row 4 P15 [19, 15, 19], (k8, p8) to last 7 [11, 7, 11] sts, p7 [11, 7, 11].

Row 5–8 As rows 1–4.

Rows 9 and 10 As rows 1 and 2.

Row 11 K15 [19, 15, 19], *p2, yb, sl4, yfwd, sl same 4 sts back onto left hand needle, yb, sl4, yfwd—referred to as bind 4, p2, k8; rep from * to last 7 [11, 7, 11] sts, k7 [11, 7, 11].

Row 12 P14 [18, 14, 18], *cr3r, p4, cr3l, p6; rep from * to last 8 [12, 8, 12] sts, p8 [12, 8, 12].

Row 13 K14 [18, 14, 18], (p2, k6) to last 8 [12, 8, 12] sts, k8 [12, 8, 12].

Row 14 P13 [17, 13, 17], (cr3r, p6, cr3l, p4) to last 9 [13, 9, 13] sts, p9 [13, 9, 13].

Row 15 K13 [17, 13, 17], (p2, k8, p2, bind 4) to last 25 [29, 25, 29] sts, p2, k8, p2, k13 [17, 13, 17].

Row 16 P13 [17, 13, 17], k2, (p8, c4f, c4b) to last 23 [27, 23, 27] sts, p8, k2, p13 [17, 13, 17].

Row 17 K13 [17, 13, 17], p2, (k8, p8) to last 23 [27, 23, 27] sts, k8, p2, k13 [17, 13, 17].

Row 18 P13 [17, 13, 17], k2, (p8, k8) to last 23 [27, 23, 27] sts, p8, k2, p13 [17, 13, 17].

Row 19 As row 17.

Rows 20–23 As rows 16–19.

Row 24 As row 16.

Row 25 As row 15.

Row 26 P13 [17, 13, 17], (cr3l, p6, cr3r, p4) to last 9 [13, 9, 13] sts, p9 [13, 9, 13].

Row 27 As row 13.

Row 28 P14 [18, 14, 18], (cr3l, p4, cr3r, p6) to last 8 [12, 8, 12] sts, p8 [12, 8, 12].

Row 29 As row 11.

Rows 2–29 form bodice patt.

Cont in bodice patt until 4 patt reps in all have been worked, ending with row 29.

Rows 2–5 of bodice form yoke patt**.

Cont in yoke patt, work 4 rows.

Shape armholes

Bind off 6 sts at beg of next 2 rows. Dec 1 st at each end of next row and every foll alt row until 124 [124, 132, 140] sts rem. Cont straight until armholes measure [8, 8¼, 8¼] inches (20 [20, 21, 21]cm), ending with a wrong-side row.

Shape shoulders

Bind off 9 [9, 9, 10] sts at beg of next 6 rows

and 8 [8, 10, 11] sts at beg of foll 2 rows. Bind off rem 54 [54, 58, 58] sts.

POCKET LINING

Using larger needles, cast on 20 sts. Beg with a k row, work 2 inches (5cm) in St st, ending with a p row.
Next row (K2, inc in next st, k2) to end. *24 sts.* Leave these sts on a spare needle.

FRONT

Work as given for back to **. Cont in yoke patt.
Divide for neck opening
Next row Patt 72 [76, 79, 83], bind off next 6 [6, 8, 8] sts, patt to end. Complete right side of front first. Patt 4 rows.
Shape armhole
Bind off 6 sts at beg of next row. Dec 1 st at armhole edge on next row and every foll alt row until 59 [59, 62, 66] sts rem. Cont straight until armhole measures 5½ [5½, 6, 6] inches (14 [14, 15, 15]cm), ending at neck edge.
Shape neck
Bind off 12 sts at beg of next row. Dec 1 st at neck edge on every row until 35 [35, 37, 41] sts rem. Cont straight until front

matches back to shoulder, ending at armhole edge.
Shape shoulder
Bind off 9 sts at beg of next row and 2 foll alt rows. Work 1 row. Bind off rem 8 [8, 10, 11] sts. With wrong side facing, rejoin yarn to rem sts and patt to end. Patt 3 rows.
Shape armhole
Bind off 6 sts at beg of next row. Dec 1 st at armhole edge on foll 4 alt rows. *62 [66, 69, 73] sts.*
Place pocket
Next row Patt 17 [17, 24, 24], sl next 24 sts onto a stitch holder and leave at back, patt across pocket lining, patt to end. Cont to dec at armhole edge on next row and every foll alt row until 59 [59, 62, 66] sts rem. Complete to match right side of front.

SLEEVES

Using smaller needles, cast on 54 sts.
Row 1 (Wrong side) K1, *p4, k1, (p1, k1) twice, p4; rep from * 3 times, k1.
Row 2 K1, *c4b, p1, (k1, p1) twice, c4f; rep from * 3 times, k1.
Row 3 As row 1.
Row 4 K1, *k4, p1, (k1, p1) twice, k4; rep from * 3 times, k1.
Rep these 4 rows 7 times, then work rows 1–3 once.
Next row Inc in first st, *k4, inc in next st, (k1, inc in next st) twice, k4; rep from * 3 times, inc in last st. 68 sts.
Change to larger needles. Begin patt.
Row 1 K1, p1, (p4, k8, p4) 4 times, p1, k1.
Row 2 K2 (c4b, p8, c4f) 4 times, k2.
Row 3 As row 1.
Row 4 K2, (k4, p8, k4) 4 times, k2.
These 4 rows form patt. Cont in patt, inc 1 st at each end of 2nd and every foll 4th row until there are 114 [122, 122, 130] sts, working extra sts into patt. Cont straight until sleeve measures 17¼ [17¾, 18, 18½] inches (44 [45, 46, 47]cm) from beg, ending with a wrong-side row.
Shape top

Bind off 6 sts at beg of next 2 rows. Dec 1 st at each end of next row and every foll alt row until 86 [102, 94, 110] sts rem, then on every row to 40 sts. Bind off 4 sts at beg of next 6 rows. Bind off rem 16 sts.

NECKBAND

Join shoulder seams. With right side facing and using smaller needles, pick up and k 30 sts up right side of neck, 44 [44, 48, 48] sts across back neck, 30 sts down left side of neck. *104 [104, 108, 108] sts.*
Row 1 (Wrong side) K1, p2, (k2, p2) to last st, k1.
Row 2 K3, (p2, k2) to last st, k1.
Rep these 2 rows 3 times, then rep row 1 again. Bind off in rib.

BUTTON BANDS

Buttonhole band
With right side facing and using smaller needles, pick up and k 40 sts evenly along right side of neck opening. Beg with a first row, work 3 rows in rib as given for neckband.
Buttonhole row Rib 6, (bind off 2, rib 8 including st used in binding off) 3 times, bind off 2, rib to end.
Next row Rib to end, casting on 2 sts over those bound off in previous row.
Rib 4 rows. Bind off in rib.
Button band
Work as given for buttonhole band but picking up sts along left side of neck opening and omitting buttonholes.

POCKET EDGINGS

With right side facing and using smaller needles, rejoin yarn to the 24 sts left on holder. Beg with a row, work 8 rows as given for neckband. Bind off in rib.

FINISHING

Block each piece as given on page 139. Catch down pocket lining and sides of pocket edging. Lap buttonhole band over button band and catch down at base of opening. Sew in sleeves. Join side and sleeve seams. Sew on buttons.

Fountain Lace Short-Sleeve Sweater

❋ MATERIALS

Yarn

4 [4, 4, 4] x 100g (3½oz) balls Patons 100% mercerized cotton 4-ply (361 yards [330m]), shade 1692 Cream

Needles and Notions

1 pair size 2 (2.75mm); 1 pair size 3 (3.25mm); Crochet hook size C/2 (2.75mm) 4 buttons, ⅝ inch (1.5cm) in diameter

Special abbreviations

c6f Sl next 3 sts onto cable needle and leave at front of work, k3 from left-hand needle, k3 from cable needle

c6b Sl next 3 sts onto cable needle and leave at back of work, k3 from left-hand needle, k3 from cable needle

ch Chain; **sc** Single crochet

❋ MEASUREMENTS

To fit chest 32 [34, 36, 38] inches (81 [86, 91, 97]cm)

Actual chest size 34¾ [36¼, 38¼, 40¼] inches (88 [92, 97, 102]cm)

Length to back neck 20 [20½, 20½, 20¾] inches (51 [52, 52, 53]cm)

Sleeve seam 3½ inches (9cm)

Gauge

28 sts and 36 rows measure 4 inches (10cm) over stockinette stitch on size 3 (3.25mm) needles (or size needed to obtain given gauge)

BACK

Using smaller needles, cast on 101 [105, 109, 115] sts.

Row 1 (Right side) K1 tbl, (p1, k1 tbl) to end.

Row 2 P1, (k1 tbl, p1) to end.

Rep these 2 rows until rib measures 2¼ inches (6cm), ending with row 1.

Next row Rib 3 [2, 1, 1], (inc in next st, rib 2) to last 5 [4, 3, 3] sts, inc in next st, rib to end. *133 [139, 145, 153] sts.*

Change to larger needles. Begin patt.

Row 1 (P2, k2) 3 [3, 3, 4] times, p2, *k9, p2 [3, 4, 4], k1, k2 tog, yo, k2, k2 tog, yo, k1, yo, sl 1, k2 tog, psso, yo, k1, yo, k2 tog, k2, yo, k2 tog tbl, k1, p2 [3, 4, 4]; rep from * twice, k9, p2, (k2, p2) 3 [3, 3, 4] times.

Row 2 (K2, p2) 3 [3, 3, 4] times, k2, *p9, k2 [3, 4, 4], p19, k2 [3, 4, 4] times; rep from * twice, p9, k2, (p2, k2) 3 [3, 3, 4] times.

Row 3 (K2, p2) 3 [3, 3, 4] times, p2, *c6f, k3, p2 [3, 4, 4], k1, k2 tog, (k3, yo, k2 tog, yo) twice, k3, k2 tog tbl, k1, p2 [3, 4, 4]; rep from * twice, c6f, k3, p2, (p2, k2) 3 [3, 3, 4] times.

Row 4 (P2, k2) 3 [3, 3, 4] times, k2, *p9, k2 [3, 4, 4], p19, k2 [3, 4, 4]; rep from * twice, p9, k2, (k2, p2) 3 [3, 3, 4] times.

Row 5 (P2, k2) 3 [3, 3, 4] times, p2, *k9, p2 [3, 4, 4], k1, k2 tog, (k2, yo) twice, k2 tog, k1, k2 tog, (yo, k2) twice, k2 tog tbl, k1, p2 [3, 4, 4]; rep from * twice, k9, p2, (k2, p2) 3 [3, 3, 4] times.

Row 6 (K2, p2) 3 [3, 3, 4] times, k2, *p9, k2 [3, 4, 4], p19, k2 [3, 4, 4]; rep from * twice, p9, k2, (p2, k2) 3 [3, 3, 4] times.

Row 7 (K2, p2) 3 [3, 3, 4] times, p2, * k3, c6b, p2 [3, 4, 4], k1, k2 tog, k1, yo, k3, yo, k2 tog, k1, k2 tog, yo, k3, yo, k1, k2 tog tbl, k1, p2 [3, 4, 4]; rep from * twice, k3, c6b, p2, (p2, k2) 3 [3, 3, 4] times.

Row 8 (P2, k2) 3 [3, 3, 4] times, k2, *p9, k2 [3, 4, 4], p19, k2 [3, 4, 4]; rep from * twice, p9, k2, (k2, p2) 3 [3, 3, 4] times.

These 8 rows form patt. Cont in patt until work measures 12½ [13, 13, 13½] inches (32 [33, 33, 34]cm) from beg, ending with a wrong-side row.

Shape armholes

Keeping continuity of patt, bind off 6 sts at beg of next 2 rows. Dec 1 st at each end of next row and every foll alt row until 109 [115, 121, 121] sts rem. **Cont straight until armholes measure 3½ inches (9cm), ending with a wrong-side row.

Divide for back neck opening

Next row Patt 55 [58, 61, 61] sts and turn; leave rem sts on a spare needle. Complete right side of neck first. Cont straight until armhole measures 7½ inches (19cm), ending at neck edge.

Shape neck and shoulder

Next row Bind off 12, patt to end.

Next row Bind off 7 [8, 8, 8], patt to last 2 sts, k2 tog.

Next row K2 tog, patt to end.

Rep last 2 rows 3 times. Bind off rem 7 [6, 9, 9] sts. With right side facing, rejoin yarn to rem sts, cast on 1, patt to end. Complete as given for first side of neck.

FRONT

Work as given for back to **. Cont straight until armholes measure 6 inches (15cm), ending with a wrong-side row.

Shape neck

Next row Patt 45 [48, 51, 51] sts, bind off 19, patt to end.

Complete right side of neck first. Dec 1 st at neck edge on every row until 35 [38, 41, 41] sts rem. Cont straight until front matches back to shoulder, ending at armhole edge.

Shape shoulder

Bind off 7 [8, 8, 8] sts at beg of next row and 3 foll alt rows. Work 1 row. Bind off rem 7 [6, 9, 9] sts. With wrong side facing, rejoin yarn to rem sts and patt to end. Complete as given for first side of neck.

SLEEVES

Using smaller needles, cast on 75 sts. Work ¾ inch (2cm) in rib as given for back waistband, ending with row 1.

Next row Rib 3, (inc in next st, rib 2) to end. *99 sts.*

Change to larger needles. Begin patt.

Row 1 P1, *k1, k2 tog, yo, k2, k2 tog, yo, k1, yo, sl 1, k2 tog, psso, yo, k1, yo, k2 tog, k2, yo, k2 tog tbl, k1, p4, k9, p4; rep from * once, k1, k2 tog, yo, k2, k2 tog, yo, k1, yo, sl 1, k2 tog, psso, yo, k1, yo, k2 tog, k2, yo, k2 tog tbl, k1, p4.

Row 2 K4, *p19, k4, p9, k4; rep from * once, p19, k4.

Row 3 P4, *k1, k2 tog, (k3, yo, k2 tog, yo) twice, k3, k2 tog tbl, k1, p4, c6f, k3, p4; rep from * once, k1, k2 tog, (k3, yo, k2 tog, yo) twice, k3, k2 tog tbl, k1, p4.

Row 4 As row 2.

Row 5 P4, *k1, k2 tog, (k2, yo) twice, k2 tog, k1, k2 tog, (yo, k2) twice, k2 tog tbl, k1, p4, k9, p4; rep from * once, k1, k2 tog, (k2, yo) twice, k2 tog, k1, k2 tog, (yo, k2) twice, k2 tog tbl, k1, p4.

Row 6 As row 2.

Row 7 P4, *k1, k2 tog, k1, yo, k3, yo, k2 tog, k1, k2 tog, yo, k3, yo, k1, k2 tog tbl, k1, p4, k3, c6b, p4; rep from * once, k1, k2 tog, k1, yo, k3, yo, k2 tog, k1, k2 tog, yo, k3, yo, k1, k2 tog tbl, k1, p4.

Row 8 As row 3.

These 8 rows form patt. Cont in patt until sleeve measures 3½ inches (9cm) from beg, ending with a wrong-side row.

Shape top

Keeping continuity of patt, bind off 6 sts at beg of next 2 rows. Dec 1 st at each end of next row and every foll alt row until 51 sts

rem, ending with a wrong-side row. Bind off 3 sts at beg of next 8 rows. Bind off rem 27 sts.

COLLAR

With right side facing, using hook and beg at right corner of neck opening, fasten yarn to edge, yo hook and draw loop through (ch made); work 52 sc (hook into next st, yo, draw loop through, yo, draw through 2 loops) to left corner, turn. Ch 1, (1 sc into next 2 sc, ch 4, skip next 4 sc), rep 3 times, 2 sc, fasten off. Join shoulder seams. With right side of back facing, using smaller needles, pick up and k 20 sts up left back neck and 38 sts down left front neck to center.

Row 1 (K1 tbl, p1) to end. This row forms rib.

Row 2 Rib 34 and turn.

Row 3 Sl 1, rib 9 and turn.

Row 4 Sl 1, rib 15 and turn.

Row 5 Sl 1, rib 21 and turn.

Row 6 Sl 1, rib 27 and turn.

Row 7 Sl 1, rib 33 and turn.

Row 8 Sl 1, rib 39 and turn.

Row 9 Sl 1, rib 45 and turn.

Row 10 Sl 1, rib 51 and turn.

Row 11 Sl 1, rib to end.

Cont in rib across all sts for another 1¼ inches (3cm). Bind off in rib. With right side facing, using smaller needles and beg at center front, pick up and k 38 sts up right front neck and 20 sts down right back neck. Complete as first side.

FINISHING

Block as given on page 139. Join side and sleeve seams. Sew in sleeves. Sew on buttons.

Classic Cotton Crewneck

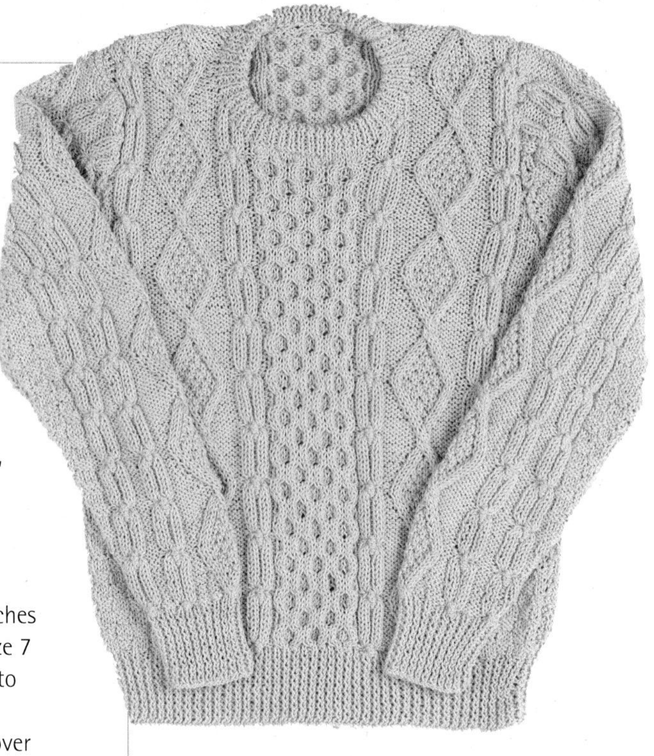

❊ MATERIALS

Yarn

7 [8, 9] x 100g (3½oz) balls Patons 100% mercerized cotton Double Knitting (230 yards [210m]), shade 2702 Sky

Needles

1 pair size 5 (3.75mm)
1 pair size 7 (4.5mm)
2 cable needles

Special abbreviations

c6 Sl next 2 sts onto first cable needle and leave at back, sl next 2 sts onto 2nd cable needle and leave at front, k2, p2 from cable needle at front, k2 from cable needle at back
c4f Sl next 2 sts onto cable needle and leave at front of work, k2 from left-hand needle, k2 from cable needle
c4b Sl next 2 sts onto cable needle and leave at back of work, k2 from left-hand needle, k2 from cable needle
cr3r Sl next st onto cable needle and leave at back of work, k2 from left-hand needle, p1 from cable needle
cr3l Sl next 2 sts onto cable needle and leave at front of work, p1 from left-hand needle, k2 from cable needle

❊ MEASUREMENTS

To fit chest 34 [36, 38] inches (86 [91, 97]cm)
Actual chest size 38½ [41, 43¼] inches (98 [104, 110]cm)
Length from back neck 23¾ [24½, 25¼] inches (60 [62, 64]cm)
Sleeve seam 17¼ [18, 19] inches (44 [46, 48]cm)

Gauge

19 sts and 27 rows measure 4 inches (10cm) over basket pattern on size 7 (4.5mm) needles (or size needed to obtain given gauge)
30 sts measure 4 inches (10cm) over honeycomb pattern on size 7 (4.5mm) needles (or size needed to obtain given gauge)

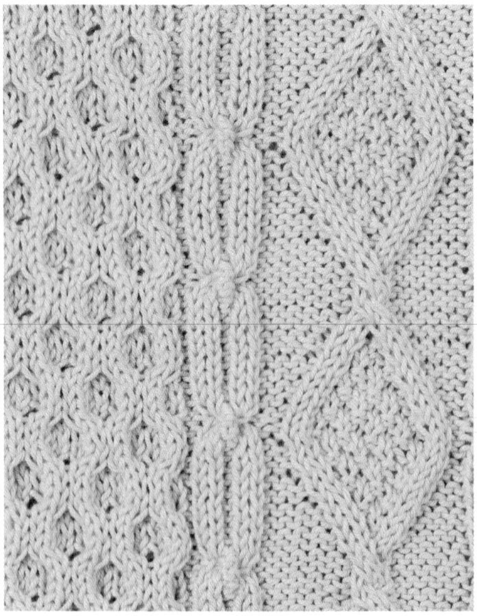

BACK

Using smaller needles, cast on 88 [92, 96] sts.
Work 2¾ inches (7cm) in k1 tbl, p1 rib.
Next row Rib 3 [2, 1], (inc in next st, rib 2) to last 4 [3, 2] sts, inc in next st, rib to end. *116 [122, 128] sts.*
Change to larger needles. Begin patt.
Row 1 (Wrong side) P0 [3, 3], (k3, p3) twice, k0 [0, 1], *(k2, p2) twice, k7 [7, 8], p4, k7 [7, 8], (p2, k2) twice*, p24; rep from * to * once, k0 [0, 1], (p3, k3) twice, p0 [3, 3].
Row 2 K0 [3, 3], (p3, k3) twice, p0 [0, 1], *p2, c6, p7 [7, 8], c4f, p7 [7, 8], c6, p2*, (c4b, c4f) 3 times; rep from * to * once, p0 [0, 1], (k3, p3) twice, k0 [3, 3].
Row 3 As row 1.
Row 4 P0 [3, 3], (k3, p3) twice, p0 [0, 1], *(p2, k2) twice, p6 [6, 7], cr3r, cr3l, p6 [6, 7], (k2, p2) twice*, k24; rep from * to * once, p0 [0, 1], (p3, k3) twice, p0 [3, 3].
Row 5 K0 [3, 3], (p3, k3) twice, k0 [0, 1], *(k2, p2) twice, k6 [6, 7], p2, k1, p3, k6 [6, 7], (p2, k2) twice*, p24; rep from * to * once, k0 [0, 1], (k3, p3) twice, k0 [3, 3].
Row 6 P0 [3, 3], (k3, p3) twice, p0 [0, 1], *(p2, k2) twice, p5 [5, 6], cr3r, k1, p1, cr3l, p5 [5, 6], (k2, p2) twice*, (c4f, c4b) 3 times; rep from * to * once, p0 [0, 1], (p3, k3) twice, p0 [3, 3].
These 6 rows establish Basket patt at each side.
Row 7 P0 [3, 3], (k3, p3) twice, k0 [0, 1], *(k2, p2) twice, k5 [5, 6], p2, (k1, p1) twice, p2, k5 [5, 6], (p2, k2) twice*, p24; rep from * to * once, k0 [0, 1], (p3, k3) twice, p0 [3, 3].
Row 8 K0 [3, 3], (p3, k3) twice, p0 [0, 1], *(p2, k2) twice, p4 [4, 5], cr3r, (k1, p1) twice, cr3l, p4 [4, 5], (k2, p2) twice*, k24; rep from * to * once, p0 [0, 1], (k3, p3) twice, k0 [3, 3].
These 8 rows establish Honeycomb patt at center.
Row 9 P0 [3, 3], (k3, p3) twice, k0 [0, 1], *(K2, p2) twice, k4 [4, 5], p2, (k1, p1) 3 times, p2, k4 [4, 5], (p2, k2) twice*, p24; rep from * to *

once, k0 [0, 1], (p3, k3) twice, p0 [3, 3].
Row 10 P0 [3, 3], (k3, p3) twice, p0 [0, 1], *(p2, k2) twice, p3 [3, 4], cr3r, (k1, p1) 3 times, cr3l, p3 [3, 4], (k2, p2) twice*, (c4b, c4f) 3 times; rep from * to * once, p0 [0, 1], (p3, k3) twice, p0 [3, 3].
Row 11 K0 [3, 3], (p3, k3) twice, k0 [0, 1], *(k2, p2) twice, k3 (3, 4], p2, (k1, p1) 4 times, p2, k3 [3, 4], (p2, k2) twice*, p24; rep from * to * once, k0 [0, 1], (k3, p3) twice, k0 [3, 3].
Row 12 P0 [3, 3], (k3, p3) twice, p0 [0, 1], *(p2, k2) twice, p2 [2, 3], cr3r, (k1, p1) 4 times, cr3l, p2 [2, 3], (k2, p2) twice*, k24; rep from * to * once, p0 [0, 1], (p3, k3) twice, p0 [3, 3].
These 12 rows establish cable patt at each side of Diamond patt.
Row 13 P0 [3, 3], (k3, p3) twice, k0 [0, 1], *(k2, p2) twice, k2 [2, 3], p2, (k1, p1) 5 times, p2, k2 [2, 3], (p2, k2) twice*, p24; rep from * to * once, k0 [0, 1], (p3, k3) twice, p0 [3, 3].
Row 14 K0 [3, 3], (p3, k3) twice, p0 [0, 1], *p2, c6, p2 [2, 3], cr3l, (p1, k1) 4 times, cr3r, p2 [2, 3], c6, p2*, (c4f, c4b) 3 times; rep from * to * once, p0 [0, 1], (k3, p3) twice, k0 [3, 3].
Row 15 P0 [3, 3], (k3, p3) twice, k0 [0, 1], *(k2, p2) twice, k3 [3, 4], p2, (k1, p1) 4 times, p2, k3 [3, 4], (p2, k2) twice*, p24; rep from * to * once, k0 [0, 1], (p3, k3) twice, p0 [3, 3].
Row 16 P0 [3, 3], (k3, p3) twice, p0 [0, 1], *(p2, k2) twice, p3 [3, 4], cr3l, (p1, k1) 3 times, cr3r, p3 [3, 4], (k2, p2) twice*, k24; rep from * to * once, p0 [0, 1], (p3, k3) twice, p0 [3, 3].
Row 17 K0 [3, 3], (p3, k3) twice, k0 [0, 1], *(k2, p2) twice, k4 [4, 5], p2, (k1, p1) 3 times, p2, k4 [4, 5], (p2, k2) twice*, p 24; rep from * to * once, k0 [0, 1], (k3, p3) twice, k0 [3, 3].
Row 18 P0 [3, 3], (k3, p3) twice, p0 [0, 1], *(p2, k2) twice, p4 [4, 5], cr3l, (p1, k1) twice, cr3r, p4 [4, 5], (k2, p2) twice*, (c4b, c4f) 3 times; rep from * to * once, p0 [0, 1], (p3, k3) twice, p0 [3, 3].
Row 19 As row 7.
Row 20 K0 [3, 3], (p3, k3) twice, p0 [0, 1], *(p2, k2) twice, p5 [5, 6], cr3l, p1, k1, cr3r, p5 [5, 6], (k2, p2) twice*, k24; rep from * to * once, p0 [0, 1], (p3, k3) twice, k0 [3, 3].
Row 21 P0 [3, 3], (k3, p3) twice, k0 [0, 1], *(k2, p2) twice, k6 [6, 7], p2, k1, p3, k6 [6, 7], (p2, k2) twice*, p24; rep from * to * once, k0 [0, 1], (p3, k3) twice, p0 [3, 3].

Row 22 P0 [3, 3], (k3, p3) twice, p0 [0, 1], *(p2, k2) twice, p6 [6, 7], cr3l, cr3r, p6 [6, 7], (k2, p2) twice*, (c4f, c4b) 3 times; rep from * to * once, p0 [0, 1], (p3, k3) twice, p0 [3, 3].
Row 23 K0 [3, 3], (p3, k3) twice, k0 [0, 1], *(k2, p2) twice, k7 [7, 8], p4, k7 [7, 8], (p2, k2) twice*, p 24; rep from * to * once, k0 [0, 1], (k3, p3) twice, k0 [3, 3].
Row 24 P0 [3, 3], (k3, p3) twice, p0 [0, 1], *(p2, k2) twice, p7 [7, 8], c4f, p7 [7, 8], (k2, p2) twice*, k24; rep from * to * once, p0 [0, 1], (p3, k3) twice, p0 [3, 3].
These 24 rows form patt. Cont in patt until work measures 15¼ [15¾, 16] inches (39 [40, 41]cm), ending with a wrong-side row.
Shape armholes
Bind off 4 sts at beg of next 2 rows. Dec 1 st at each end of next row and every foll alt row until 92 [94, 98] sts rem. Cont straight until armholes measure 17½ [8, 8¼] inches (19 [20, 21]cm), ending with a wrong-side row.
Shape shoulders
Bind off 6 [7, 7] sts at beg of next 6 rows and 8 [6, 8] sts at beg of foll 2 rows. Bind off rem 40 sts.

FRONT

Work as given for back until armholes measure 4¼ [4¾, 5] inches (11 [12, 13]cm), ending with a wrong-side row.
Shape neck
Next row Patt 34 [35, 37] sts and turn; leave rem sts on a spare needle. Complete left side of neck first. Dec 1 st at neck edge on next 8 rows. *26 [27, 29] sts.*
Cont straight until front matches back to shoulder, ending at armhole edge.
Shape shoulder
Bind off 6 [7, 7] sts at beg of next row and foll 2 alt rows. Patt 1 row. Bind off rem 8 [6, 8] sts. With right side facing, rejoin yarn to rem sts, bind off first 24 sts, patt to end. Complete as given for left side of neck.

SLEEVES

Using smaller needles, cast on 42 [44, 46] sts. Work 2¾ inches (7cm) k1 tbl, p1 rib.
Next row Rib 1 [2, 3], (inc in next st, rib 2) to last 2 [3, 4] sts, inc in next st, rib to end.

56 [58, 60] sts.
Change to larger needles. Begin patt.
Row 1 (Wrong side) P0 [1, 2], (k2, p2) twice, k2, now rep row 1 as given for 3rd size on back from * to * once, k2, (p2, k2) twice, p0 [1, 2].
Row 2 K0 [1, 2], p2, c6, p2, now rep row 2 as given for 3rd size on back from * to * once, p2, c6, p2, k0 [1, 2].
Row 3 P0 [1, 2], (k2, p2) twice, k2, now rep row 3 as given for 3rd size on back from * to * once, k2, (p2, k2) twice, p0 [1, 2].
Row 4 P0 [1, 2], (p2, k2) twice, p2, now rep row 4 as given for 3rd size on back from * to * once, p2, (k2, p2) twice, p0 [1, 2].
Row 5 K0 [1, 2], (k2, p2) twice, k2, now rep row 5 as given for 3rd size on back from * to * once, k2, (p2, k2) twice, k0 [1, 2].
Row 6 P0 [1, 2], (p2, k2) twice, p2, now rep row 6 as given for 3rd size on back from * to * once, p2, (k2, p2) twice, p0 [1, 2].
These 6 rows establish patt for sleeve. Cont in patt as set, working appropriate rows of Diamond and cable patt and working additional cable at each side of center panel. Inc 1 st at each end of next row and every foll 5th row until there are 86 [90, 94] sts, working extra sts into Basket patt. Cont straight until sleeve measures 17¼ [18, 19] inches (44 [46, 48]cm), ending with wrong-side row.
Shape top
Bind off 4 sts at beg of next 2 rows. Dec 1 st at each end of next row and every foll alt row until 58 [58, 62] sts rem, then on every row to 40 sts. Bind off.

NECKBAND

Join right shoulder seam. With right side facing and using smaller needles, pick up and k 21 sts down left side of neck, 16 sts across center front, 21 sts up right side of neck, 36 sts across back neck. *94 sts.* Work 2¼ inches (6cm) in k1 tbl, p1 rib. Bind off in rib.

FINISHING

Block as given on page 139. Join left shoulder and neckband seam. Fold neckband in half to wrong side and slipstitch in place. Join side and sleeve seams. Sew in sleeves.

Shetland Lace

Along with the multicolored knitting of Fair Isle, the Shetland Islands have produced world-famous lace knitting, which originated in the most northerly of the islands, Unst. The "ring" shawls, knitted from 1-ply lace wool, were highly prized, and could take a whole winter to complete. So fine was the hand-spun wool that 2 ounces of fleece could produce 6,000 yards of yarn; and the finished shawl was so delicate that, although measuring perhaps 6 feet square, it could be pulled through a wedding ring. The patterns were handed from mother to daughter, and combined traditional motifs such as Tree of Life, Spider's Web, Cat's Paw, and Horseshoe. A lace shawl would be worn as a bridal veil, and then used for christenings; black shawls would be worn for mourning. These are now museum pieces, and very few knitters remain who have the skill to knit them.

Commercial lace knitting in Shetland started around 1830 in order to provide employment when the first knitting machines, which could produce only a plain fabric, were introduced. The rise of this cottage industry was quite rapid, but it lasted only until the end of the nineteenth century. In order to popularize their lace, in 1837 the Shetland knitters presented Queen Victoria and the Duchess of Kent with fine lace stockings; shortly after this, a hosiery dealer introduced Shetland lace to the London market. Lace-knit underwear, stockings, and children's dresses became much in demand, and every lady of fashion had Shetland lace in her wardrobe. A fine lace wedding veil was shown at London's Great Exhibition, in the Crystal Palace, in 1851, where the craftsmanship was greatly admired.

One of the reasons for the success of Shetland lace is the quality of the wool. The Shetland sheep is a small, hardy and ancient breed; its wool has a long staple and is very fine and soft. In the summer, the fleece becomes loose naturally and can be plucked away, or "rooed," by hand. The hand-spun lace yarn used only the finest part of the fleece, from the animal's neck, making the lace light and delicate, but also warm.

The Shetland women themselves wore the plainer Shetland shawls, or "haps," knitted with ordinary wool, often in the undyed shades, with just a little openwork pattern in their striped borders. These were part of the women's dress and would be worn with the corners crossed over the chest and tied at the back of the waist. This enabled the woman to walk around with her hands free to bring in the peat—or indeed to do her knitting.

The construction of the shawls is interesting. They are knitted from the edge inward, with as many edges as possible picked up from other edges, so that there are very few seams; those that do exist are made with a special technique in which the needle join imitates the join made with knitting. The finished shawl would be washed carefully and then "dressed" by being strung onto a frame. In this technique, a thread is passed through the tip of each lace point and then around each of the numerous wooden pegs around the frame. After drying naturally, the shawl appears pressed to a perfect shape. The same process can be repeated when the shawl next needs washing.

As the Victorian era came to an end, so did the demand for Shetland lace. There was a brief revival during the Second World War, when machine-made lace from Nottingham was not available because its factories were turned over to the production of munitions, and the Shetland knitters produced little lacy pullovers and cardigans to satisfy the demand. These garments—now so evocative of the 1940s—were often bought by servicemen stationed in the Shetlands, who then sent them home to their wives and sweethearts.

All the patterns here are the traditional patterns knitted in Shetland for more than a hundred years; the one adaptation we have made is the New Shell Tunic, which uses a traditional scarf stitch converted to a T-shaped garment in a sweater-weight yarn. Enjoy the warmth of Shetland wool and the soft colors of a very special area of Britain-these patterns capture a timeless style that is still totally wearable today.

New Shell Pattern Lace Sweater

This easy-to-knit pattern, with its pointed chevron effect, was traditionally used for fine lace scarves; here it has been adapted to the sweater-weight Shetland wool. The delicate pointed edging finishes the sleeves and hem prettily.

Lace Cardigan in Eyelet Pattern

A traditional Shetland eyelet pattern is worked in 2-ply lace wool to make a gossamer-fine openwork cardigan, suitable for a summer evening. It is knitted in the round up to the armholes, making a virtually seam-free garment in this soft, light wool.

Old Shell Pattern Lace Sweater

This delicate openwork sweater is made from 2-ply Shetland lace wool. The shaded stripes of the natural colors of the famous Shetland sheep, combined with the lovely Old Shell pattern, make a timeless and classic sweater.

Fern Motif Sweater

Based on a traditional British undershirt called a spencer, this pretty sweater contrasts garter stitch with a fern motif. Shown here in soft merino wool, it makes an easy-to-wear top for a spring day. It is knitted in one piece up to the armholes, then the front edges are slipstitched neatly together.

Old Shell Shetland Shawl

The Shetland Islands have long been famous for their shawls. The everyday versions often had borders using all the shades of the natural undyed wool. The border of this one features the Old Shell pattern and a pointed lace edging. It makes a cozy wrap or pretty throw and is both light and warm.

New Shell Pattern Lace Sweater

❋ MATERIALS

Yarn

Jamieson's Spindrift 2-ply (100%
Shetland wool, approx 115 yards [105m])
A 5 [5, 5] x 25g (⅞oz) balls, shade 769 Willow
B 2 [2, 2] x 25g balls, shade 821 Rosemary
C 2 [2, 2] x 25g balls, shade 547 Orchid
D 1 [2, 2] x 25g balls, shade 562 Cyclamen
E 1 [1, 1] x 25g balls, shade 794 Eucalyptus
F 1 [1, 2] x 25g balls, shade 603 Pot-pourri

Needles

1 pair size 5 (3.75mm)
1 pair size 1 (2.25mm)

Notions

2 stitch holders

❋ MEASUREMENTS

To fit chest 30 [32, 34] inches
(76 [81, 86]cm)
Actual chest size 32¼ [35½, 38½] inches
(82 [90, 98]cm)
Length from back neck 22 [22¾, 23½]
inches (56 [58, 60]cm)
Sleeve seam 19 inches (48cm)

Gauge

24 sts and 25 rows measure 4 inches
(10cm) over pattern on size 5 (3.75mm)
needles (or size needed to obtain
given gauge)

BACK

Using larger needles and yarn B, cast
on 101 [111, 121] sts. **Begin patt.
Row 1 (Right side) K1, (yo, k3, k3 tog, k3, yo,
k1) to end.
Row 2 Knit.
These 2 rows form patt. Cont in patt and color
sequence as follows: 8 rows in B, 2 rows in F,
4 rows in E, 4 rows in C, (2 rows in A, 2 rows
in D) 3 times, 2 rows in A, 8 rows in B, 4
rows in D, (2 rows in C, 2 rows in F) 3 times,
2 rows in C, 8 rows in E, 2 rows in D, 8 rows
in C, 2 rows in B, 2 rows in C, 2 rows in B, 2
rows in D, 8 rows in A, 2 rows in F,
2 rows in A, 2 rows in F**. Cont in A
only until work measures 22 [22¾,
23¼,] inches (56 [58, 60]cm), ending
with a wrong-side row.
Shape neck
Next row Patt 37 [41, 45]
and turn; leave rem sts on
a spare needle. Complete
right side of neck first.
Dec 1 st at neck edge on
next 4 rows then on every
foll alt row until 29 [33, 37]
sts rem. Patt 1 row. Bind off.
With right side facing, sl
center 27 [29, 31] sts onto
stitch holder, rejoin yarn
to rem sts and patt to end.
Complete as given for first
side of neck.

FRONT

Work as given for back until work
measures 20½ [21¼, 22] inches (52 [54,
56]cm), ending with a wrong-side row.
Shape neck
Next row Patt 41 [45, 49] and turn; leave
rem sts on a spare needle.
Complete left side of neck first.
Dec 1 st at neck edge on next 6 rows then
on every foll alt row until 29 [33, 37] sts rem.
Cont straight until front matches back to
shoulder, ending with a wrong-side row.
Bind off.
With right side facing, sl center 19 [21, 23] sts
onto stitch holder, rejoin yarn to rem sts and patt
to end. Complete as given for first side of neck.

SLEEVES

Using larger needles and yarn B, cast on
91 [101, 101] sts. Work as given for back
from ** to **.
Work 8 rows in C, 2 rows in F, 2 rows in D,
8 rows in A. Bind off.

NECKBAND

Join right shoulder seam. With right side
facing, using smaller needles and yarn A, pick
up and k 23 sts down left front neck, k across
19 [21, 23] center front sts, pick up and k 23
sts up right front neck, 14 sts down right back
neck, k across 27 [29, 31] center back sts, pick
up and k 14 sts up left back neck.
120 [124, 128] sts.
Work 13 Rows in k1, p1 rib. Bind off in rib.

FINISHING

Block each piece as given on page 139. Join
left shoulder and neckband seam. Mark
positions of armholes 7½ [8, 8] inches (19
[20, 20]cm) down from shoulders on back
and front. Sew in sleeves between markers.
Join side and sleeve seams.

Lace Cardigan in Eyelet Pattern

POCKET LININGS

Using larger needles, cast on 21 sts. Beg
with a k row, work 24 rows in St st. Leave
these sts on a spare needle. Make another
pocket lining to match.

BACK AND FRONTS

This cardigan is knitted in one piece to the
armholes. Using smaller needles, cast on 171 sts.
Row 1 K1, (p1, k1) to end.
Row 2 P1, (k1, p1) to end.
Rep last 2 rows 14 times then row 1 again.
Next row Rib 4, (inc in next st, rib 2) to last
2 sts, rib 2. *226 sts.*
Change to larger needles. Begin patt.
Row 1 (Right side) K2, (yo, k1, k3 tog, k1,
yo, k2) to end.
Row 2 Purl.
Row 3 K3, (yo, k3 tog, yo, k4)
to last 6 sts, yo, k3 tog, yo, k3.
Row 4 Purl.
These 4 rows form patt.
Cont in patt until work
measures 6 inches
(15cm), ending with
a p row.

Place pockets

Next row Patt 8, sl next 21
sts onto a stitch holder, patt
across sts of first pocket lining,
patt to last 29 sts, sl next 21 st
onto a stitch holder, patt to end.
Cont in patt until work measures
15 inches (38cm), ending with a
row 4.

Divide for armholes

Next row K2 tog, patt 47, k2 tog and
turn; leave rem sts on a spare needle.
Complete right front first. Patt 1 row.
Dec 1 st at beg of next row and every
foll alt row until 22 sts rem. Patt 1 row.
Bind off.
With right side facing, sl next 19 sts onto a
safety pin, rejoin yarn to rem sts, k2 tog, patt
82, k2 tog and turn, leave rem sts on a spare
needle. Complete back first. Cont straight until
back matches front to shoulder, ending with
a wrong-side row. Bind off.
With right side facing, sl next 19 sts onto a
safety pin, rejoin yarn to rem sts, k2 tog, patt
to last 2 sts, k2 tog. Patt 1 row. Dec 1 st at
end of next row and every foll alt row until
22 sts rem. Patt 1 row. Bind off.

SLEEVES

Join shoulder seams. With right side facing
and using larger double-pointed needles, pick
up and k 79 sts evenly around armhole edge,
then patt across 19 sts on safety pin. Work in
rounds as follows:
Round 1 Knit.

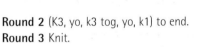

Round 2 (K3, yo, k3 tog, yo, k1) to end.
Round 3 Knit.
Round 4 (K2, yo, k1, k3 tog, k1, yo) to end.
Next round Patt 86, k2 tog, k1, k2 tog, patt
to end.
Keeping continuity of patt, work 7 rounds.
Next round Patt 85, k2 tog, k1, k2 tog, patt
to end.
Keeping continuity of patt, work 7 rounds.
Cont dec in this way on next round and 4 foll
8th rounds.
Next round Patt 80, (k2 tog, k1) twice. Sl last
2 sts of last round onto next needle.
Next round Sl 2, patt to end.
Work 6 rounds.
Next round K2 tog, patt to last 3 sts, k2 tog, k1.
Work 7 rounds.
Next round K2 tog, patt to last 3 sts, k2 tog, k1.
Rep last 8 rounds until 72 sts rem.
Work 7 rounds.
Next round (K2 tog, k1) to end. *48 sts.*

Change to smaller double-pointed needles.
Work 32 rounds in k1, p1 rib.
Bind off in rib.

FRONT BAND

Mark right front with pins to indicate
buttonholes: first one to come ⅜ inch (1cm)
up from lower edge and last one 2¾ inches
(7cm) down from beg of front shaping, rem 4
evenly spaced between. Using smaller needles,
bind on 11 sts.
Row 1 K1, (p1, k1) to end.
This row forms seed st. Cont in seed st until
band when slightly stretched fits along right
front, across back neck and down left front,
making buttonholes at pin positions as follows:
Next row (K1, p1) twice, yo, p2 tog, k1, (p1,
k1) twice. Bind off.

POCKET EDGINGS

With right side facing and using smaller
needles, rejoin yarn to the 21 sts left on stitch
holder. Work 8 rows in seed st. Bind off.

FINISHING

Block as given on page 139. Sew on front
band and buttons. Catch down pocket linings
and sides of pocket edgings.

Old Shell Pattern Lace Sweater

❖ MATERIALS

Yarn

Jamieson's Ultra 2-ply lace weight (50% lambswool/50% Shetland wool, approx 160 yards [175m])

A 5 [6, 7] x 25g (⁹⁄₁₀oz) balls, shade 103 Sholmit

B 2 [2, 2] x 25g balls, shade 101 Shetland Black

C 2 [2, 2] x 25g balls, shade 108 Moorit

D 2 [3, 3] x 25g balls, shade 105 Eesit

E 2 [2, 2] x 25g balls, shade 104 Natural White

F 2 [2, 2] x 25g balls, shade 107 Mogit

G 2 [2, 2] x 25g balls, shade 102 Shaela

Needles

1 circular needle size 1 (2.25mm), 24 inches (60cm) long; 1 circular needle size 2 (3mm), 32 inches (80cm) long; 1 set of double-pointed needles size 1 (2.25mm); 1 set of double-pointed needles size 2 (3mm); 1 pair size 1 (2.25mm)

Notions

4 buttons, ³⁄₈ inch (1cm) in diameter; 1 stitch holder

❖ MEASUREMENTS

To fit chest 30-32 [34-36, 38-40] inches (76-81 [86-91, 97-102]cm)

Actual chest size 35½ [39¾, 44] inches (90 [101, 112]cm)

Length from back neck 22¾ [24, 24¾] inches (58 [61, 63]cm)

Sleeve seam 20¾ inches (53cm)

Gauge

32 sts and 38 rows measure 4 inches (10cm) over pattern on size 2 (3mm) needles (or size needed to obtain given gauge)

BACK AND FRONT

This sweater is knitted in one piece to the armholes.

Using smaller circular needle and yarn A, cast on 264 [288, 324] sts. Work in rounds of k1, p1 rib for 2 inches (5cm).

Next round *Rib 11 [8, 9], pick up loop lying between sts and work tbl; rep from * to end. *288 [324, 360] sts.*

Change to larger circular needle.

Begin patt.

Rounds 1 and 2 Knit.

Round 3 *(K2 tog) 3 times, (yo, k1) 6 times, (k2 tog) 3 times; rep from * to end.

Round 4 Knit.

These 4 rounds form shell patt. Cont in shell patt and color sequence as follows:

Rounds 5–18 In yarn A.

Round 19 In yarn B.

Rounds 20 and 21 In yarn C.

Rounds 22 and 23 In yarn D.

Round 24 In yarn E.

Round 25 In yarn D.

Round 26 In yarn F.

Round 27 In yarn D.

Round 28 In yarn G.

Rounds 29 and 30 In yarn A.

Round 31 In yarn B.

Rounds 32 and 33 In yarn A.

Round 34 In yarn G.

Round 35 In yarn D.

Round 36 In yarn F.

Round 37 In yarn D.

Round 38 In yarn E.

Rounds 39 and 40 In yarn D.

Rounds 41 and 42 In yarn C.

Round 43 In yarn B.

Round 44 In yarn A.

These 44 rounds form color sequence.

Cont in shell patt and color sequence until work measures 15 inches (38cm), ending with round 36.

Divide for back and front

Next round *Patt 9 and sl these sts onto a safety pin, patt 126 [144, 162], patt 9 and sl these sts onto a safety pin; rep from * once. Complete back first. Keeping cont of color sequence work backward and forward as follows:

Next row Purl.

**Row 1 Bind off 2, k7, including st used in binding off, *(k2 tog) 3 times, (yo, k1) 6 times, (k2 tog) 3 times; rep from * to last 9 sts, k9.

Row 2 Bind off 2, p to end.

Row 3 Bind off 2, k to end.

Row 4 As row 2.

These 4 rows establish cont of shell patt. Keeping cont of shell patt and color sequence, bind off 2 sts at beg of next 10 rows.

Dec 1 st at each end of next row and 2 foll alt rows. *92 [110, 128] sts***.
Cont straight until armholes measure 6 [6¼, 7] inches (15 [16, 18]cm), ending with a wrong-side row.

Divide for back neck opening
Next row Patt 42 [51, 60] sts and turn; leave rem sts on a spare needle. Complete right side of back neck first.
Cont straight until armhole measures 8 [9, 9¾] inches (20 [23, 25]cm), ending at armhole edge. Leave these sts on a spare needle.
With right side of back facing, sl center 8 sts onto a safety pin, rejoin appropriate yarn to rem sts and patt to end. Complete to match first side of neck.
With wrong side of front facing, rejoin appropriate yarn to rem sts, p to end. Work as given for back from ** to **. Cont straight until armholes measure 5 [6, 6] inches (13 [15, 15]cm), ending with a wrong-side row.

Shape neck
Next row Patt 36 [45, 54] and turn; leave rem sts on a spare needle.
Complete left side of front neck first. Bind off 2 [2, 3] sts at beg of next row and 2 sts at beg of every foll alt row until 20 [29, 33] sts rem. Cont straight until front matches back to shoulder, ending at armhole edge.

Join left shoulder
With right sides of back and front facing, bind off 20 [29, 33] sts, taking 1 st from each needle and working them tog. Leave rem 22 [22, 27] sts on back neck on a spare needle.
With right side of front facing, sl center 20 sts onto a stitch holder, rejoin appropriate yarn to rem sts and patt to end. Patt 1 row. Complete as given for first side of front neck.

NECKBAND

With right side facing, using smaller circular needle and yarn A, k 22 [22, 27] sts from left back neck, pick up and k 32 [34, 38] sts down left front neck, k 20 center front sts, pick up and k 32 [34, 38] sts up right front neck and k 22 [22, 27] sts from right back neck. *128 [132, 150] sts.*
Work backward and forward in k1, p1 rib for 9 [11, 13] rows. Bind off in rib.

OPENING BANDS

Button band
With right side facing, using pair of needles and yarn A and beg at base of opening, pick up and k 26 [32, 32] sts along left edge to top of neckband.
Row 1 (Wrong side) (K1, p1) to end.
Row 2 (P1, k1) to end.
These 2 rows form seed st. Work another 9 rows in seed st. Bind off.

Buttonhole band
With right side facing and using pair of needles, rejoin yarn A to 8 sts on a safety pin at base of opening. Work 4 [6, 6] rows in seed st patt as given for button band.
Next row Seed st 3, bind off 2, seed st to end.
Next row Seed st to end, casting on 2 sts over those bound off in previous row.
Work 8 [10, 10] rows in seed st. Rep last 10 [12, 12] rows twice then the buttonhole rows again. Work 4 [6, 6] rows in seed st. Bind off. Sew buttonhole band in place. Catch down button band on wrong side of base of opening. Sew on buttons.

SLEEVES

With right side facing, using larger double-pointed needles and yarn A, k 9 sts from left-hand-side safety pin, pick up and k 108 [126, 144] sts evenly around armhole edge, k 9 from rem safety pin. *126 [144, 162] sts.*
Cont in rounds in shell patt and color sequence as given for back and front. Work 44 rounds.
Next round K1, k2 tog, patt to last 3 sts, k2 tog, k1.
Patt 7 [4, 4] rounds straight. Rep last 8 [5, 5] rounds until 90 [90, 108] sts rem. Cont straight until sleeve measures 19¼ inches (49cm). Change to smaller double-pointed needles.
Next round *K1, (k2 tog) 4 times; rep from * to end. *50 [50, 60] sts.*
Work in rounds of k1, p1 rib for 2¾ inches (7cm). Bind off in rib.

FINISHING

Block as given on page 139.

Fern Motif Sweater

❋ MATERIALS

Yarn

6 x 50g (1¾oz) balls Rowan 4-ply Soft 100% Merino wool (approx 191 yards [175m]), shade 387 Rain Cloud

Needles

1 pair size 3 (3.25mm); 1 circular needle size 3 (3.25mm), 24 inches (60cm) long

❋ MEASUREMENTS

To fit chest 32-34 inches (81-86cm)
Actual chest size 36¼ inches (92cm)
Length from back neck 55cm, 21¾in
Sleeve seam 17¾ inches (45cm)

Gauge

21 sts and 34 rows measure 4 inches (10cm) over garter st on size 3 (3.25mm) needles (or size needed to obtain given gauge)

PANEL PATTERN

Repeat of 25 sts

Row 1 Knit.
Row 2 and every foll alt row Knit.
Row 3 K10, k2 tog, yo, k1, yo, k2 tog, k10.
Row 5 K9, k2 tog, yo, k3, yo, k2 tog, k9.
Row 7 K8, (k2 tog, yo) twice, k1, (yo, k2 tog) twice, k8.
Row 9 K7, (k2 tog, yo) twice, k3, (yo, k2 tog) twice, k7.
Row 11 K6, (k2 tog, yo) 3 times, k1, (yo, k2 tog) 3 times, k6.
Row 13 K5, (k2 tog, yo) 3 times, k3, (yo, k2 tog) 3 times, k5.
Row 15 K4, (k2 tog, yo) 4 times, k1, (yo, k2 tog) 4 times, k4.
Row 17 K3, (k2 tog, yo) 4 times, k3, (yo, k2 tog) 4 times, k3.
Row 19 K2, (k2 tog, yo) 5 times, k1, (yo, k2 tog) 5 times, k2.
Row 21 As row 17.
Row 23 As row 15.
Row 25 As row 13.
Row 27 As row 11.
Row 29 As row 9.
Row 31 As row 7.
Row 33 As row 5.
Row 35 K11, yo, k3 tog, yo, k11.
Row 36 Knit.
These 36 rows form panel patt.

BACK AND FRONT

This sweater is worked in one piece to the armholes. Using pair of needles, cast on 143 sts. Knit 1 row.
Row 1 K2, (yo, k3, k3 tog, k3, yo, k1) to last st, k1.
Row 2 Knit.
These 2 rows form waistband patt. Rep these 2 rows 9 times.
Next row K15, (k2 tog, k26) 4 times, k2 tog, k14. *138 sts.*
Knit 1 row.
Next row K1, (yo, k 2 tog) to last st, yo, k1. *139 sts.*
Knit 1 row. Cont in patt as follows:
Row 1 Knit.
Row 2 and every foll alt row Knit.
Row 3 Work row 3 of panel patt, k1, yo, k16, yo, k to last 42 sts, yo, k16, yo, k1, work row 3 of panel patt.
Row 5 Work row 5 of panel patt, k to last 25 sts, work row 5 of panel patt.
Row 7 Work row 7 of panel patt, k to last 25 sts, work row 7 of panel patt.
Row 9 Work row 9 of panel patt, k to last 25 sts, work row 9 of panel patt.
Row 11 Work row 11 of panel patt, k2, yo, k16, yo, k to last 43 sts, yo, k16, yo, k2, work row 11 of panel patt.
Cont in this way, working appropriate rows of panel patt and inc sts as set on every foll 8th row until there are 195 sts. Work 1 row.

Divide for armholes

Next row K2, k2 tog, yo, k1, k2 tog, k34 and turn; leave rem sts on a spare needle. Complete right side of neck first.
Row 1 K to last 4 sts, yo, k2 tog, k2.
Row 2 K2, k2 tog, yo, k to end.
Rows 3 and 4 As rows 1 and 2.
Row 5 As row 1.
Row 6 K2, k2 tog, yo, k1, k2 tog, k to end.
Rep these 6 rows 7 times then rows 1 and 2 again. Bind off rem 32 sts.
With right side facing, sl next 15 sts onto a safety pin, rejoin yarn to rem sts, k83 and turn; leave rem sts on a spare needle. Knit 49 rows.

Shape shoulders

Bind off 28 sts at beg of next 2 rows. *27 sts.*
Next row K1, (yo, k2 tog) to end.
Knit 3 rows. Bind off.
With right side facing, sl next 15 sts onto a safety pin, rejoin yarn to rem sts, k to last 7 sts, k2 tog, k1, yo, k2 tog, k2.
Row 1 K2, k2 tog, yo, k to end.
Row 2 K to last 4 sts, yo, k2 tog, k2.
Rows 3 and 4 As rows 1 and 2.

Row 5 As row 1.
Row 6 K to last 7 sts, k2 tog, k1, yo, k2 tog, k2.
Rep these 6 rows 7 times then row 1 again.
Bind off rem 32 sts.

SLEEVES

Join shoulder and neck edge border seams.

With right side facing and using circular needle, k7 sts from safety pin, pick up and k 52 sts evenly around armhole edge, then k rem 8 sts on safety pin. *67 sts.*
Work backward and forward. K 57 rows.
Next row K2 tog, k to last 3 sts, k2 tog, k1.
K 7 rows straight. Rep last 8 rows 7 times.
Next row K2tog, k to last 3 sts, k2 tog. k1. K 3

rows straight. Rep last 4 rows 3 times. *43 sts.*
Work 12 rows in waistband patt as given for main part. Bind off.

FINISHING

Block as given on page 139. Join center front and sleeve seams.

Old Shell Shetland Shawl

❋ MATERIALS

Yarn
Jamieson and Smith's 2-ply Jumper
Weight (100% Shetland wool, approx
125 yards [115m]): A 3 x 25g (⁹⁄₁₀oz) balls,
shade FC44 (peat brown)
Jamieson's Spindrift 2-ply (100% Shetland
wool, approx 115 yards [105m])
B 3 x 25g balls, shade 319 Harris Green
C 2 x 25g balls, shade 155 Bramble
D 2 x 25g balls, shade 337 Camel

E 5 x 25g balls, shade 179 Buttermilk

Needles
1 long pair size 8 (5mm)

❋ MEASUREMENTS

Approximately 52 inches (132cm) square
Gauge
14 sts and 28 rows measure 4 inches (10cm)
over garter st on size 8 (5mm) needles (or
size needed to obtain given gauge)

Special note
This shawl is knitted in sections as follows:
Part 1 The scalloped lace edging that goes
around two sides.
Part 2 The striped border for two sides with
Old Shell pattern and with an openwork stitch
at center of rows (i.e. dividing the two sides)
and one end of the rows.
Parts 3 and 4 As parts 1 and 2, to make the
edging and border for the other two sides.
Part 5 The center panel, which is worked from
the inside edge of half of one of the border
pieces (i.e. one side of the shawl), knitting in
the other half of the same border piece, and
half of the other border piece.

SCALLOPED LACE EDGING

This is part 1 on the diagram.
Using yarn A cast on 6 sts.
Row 1 K4, yo, k2.
Row 2 K2, yo, k5.
Row 3 K6, yo, k2.
Row 4 K2, yo, k7.
Row 5 K8, yo, k2.
Row 6 K2, yo, k9. *12 sts.*
Row 7 K7, k2 tog, yo, k2 tog, k1.

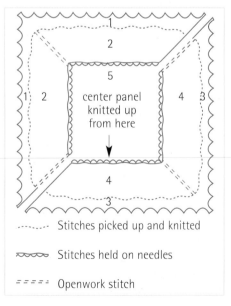

- - - - Stitches picked up and knitted

〜〜〜 Stitches held on needles

= = = = Openwork stitch

Row 8 K1, k2 tog, yo, k2 tog, k6.
Row 9 K5, k2 tog, yo, k2 tog, k1.
Row 10 K1, k2 tog, yo, k2 tog, k4.
Row 11 K3, k2 tog, yo, k2 tog, k1.
Row 12 K1, k2 tog, yo, k2 tog, k2. *6 sts.*
Rows 13 to 18 Knit.
Rep these 18 rows 28 times, then work rows 1–17.
Next row Bind off these 6 sts, but do not turn and break off yarn.

STRIPED BORDER

This is part 2 on the diagram.
Change to yarn B. Pick up and k 270 sts along straight edge of work.
Next row (Wrong side) *K2, yo, k2 tog, k5, (k2 tog, k7) 14 times; rep from * once. *242 sts.*
Begin patt. Change to yarn A.
Row 1 (K119, yo, k2 tog) twice.
Row 2 (K2, yo, k2 tog, k117) twice.
Row 3 **K6, *(k2 tog) 3 times, (yo, k1) 5 times, yo, (k2 tog) 3 times, k1, rep from * 5 times, k5, yo, k2 tog**; rep from ** to ** once.
Row 4 As row 2.
Change to yarn B.
Rows 5–8 Rep rows 1 and 2 twice.
These 8 rows form patt. Cont in patt and color sequence as follows:
2 rows in yarn B, 2 rows in yarn C, 4 rows in yarn B, 6 rows in yarn C, 2 rows in yarn D, 4 rows in yarn C, 6 rows in yarn D, 2 rows in yarn E, 4 rows in yarn D, 6 rows in yarn E, 2 rows in yarn B, 2 rows in yarn E, ending with a row 2 of the patt.
Shape border
Cont with yarn E.
Row 1 **K5, (k2 tog) 3 times, (yo, k1) 4 times, yo, (k2 tog) 4 times, *k1, (k2 tog) 3 times, (yo, k1) 5 times, yo, (k 2 tog) 3 times; rep from * 3 times more, k1, (k2 tog) 4 times, (yo, k1) 4 times, yo, (k2 tog) 3 times, k5, yo, k2 tog**; rep from ** to ** once. *234 sts.*
Row 2 (K2, yo, k2 tog, k113) twice.
Change to yarn B.
Row 3 (K115, yo, k2 tog) twice.
Row 4 As row 2.
Rows 5 to 8 Rep rows 3 and 4 twice.
Change to yarn C.
Row 9 **K4, (k2 tog) 3 times, (yo, k1) 3 times,

yo, (k2 tog) 4 times, *k1, (k2 tog) 3 times, (yo, k1) 5 times, yo, (k2 tog) 3 times; rep from * 3 times, k1, (k2 tog) 4 times, (yo, k1) 3 times, yo, (k2 tog) 3 times, k4, yo, k2 tog**; rep from ** to ** once more. *222 sts.*
Row 10 (K2, yo, k2 tog, k107) twice.
Change to yarn B.
Row 11 (K109, yo, k2 tog) twice.
Row 12 As row 10.
Rows 13 and 14 As rows 11 and 12.
Change to yarn C
Rows 15 and 16 Rep rows 11 and 12.
Row 17 **K3, (k2 tog) 3 times, (yo, k1) twice, yo, (k2 tog) twice, k3 tog, *k1, (k2 tog) 3 times, (yo, k1) 5 times, yo, (k2 tog) 3 times; rep from * 3 times more, k1, k3 tog, (k2 tog) twice, (yo, k1) twice, yo, (k2 tog) 3 times, k3, yo, k2 tog**; rep from ** to ** once. *206 sts.*
Row 18 (K2, yo, k2 tog, k99) twice.
Change to yarn F.
Row 19 (K101, yo, k2 tog) twice.
Row 20 As row 18.
Change to yarn D.
Rows 21 and 22 Rep rows 19 and 20.
Change to yarn C.
Rows 23 and 24 Rep rows 19 and 20.
Row 25 **K3, (k2 tog) 3 times, yo, k1, yo, (k2 tog) twice, *k1, (k2 tog) 3 times, (yo, k1) 5 times, yo, (k2 tog) 3 times; rep from * 3 times more, k1 (k2 tog) twice, yo, k1, yo, (k2 tog) 3 times, k3, yo, k2 tog**; rep from ** to ** once more.
Row 26 (K2, yo, k2 tog, k93) twice.
Change to yarn D.
Row 27 (K95, yo, k2 tog) twice.
Row 28 As row 26.
Rows 29–32 Rep rows 27 and 28 twice. Change to yarn E.
Row 33 **K3, (k2 tog) twice, yo, (k2 tog) twice, *k1, (k2 tog) 3 times, (yo, k1) 5 times, yo, (k2 tog) 3 times; rep from * 3 times, k1, (k2 tog) twice, yo, (k2 tog) twice, k3, yo, k2 tog**; rep from ** to ** once.
Row 34 (K2, yo, k2 tog, k87) twice.
Change to yarn D.
Row 35 (K89, yo, k2 tog) twice.
Row 36 (K2, yo, k2 tog, k42, k2 tog, k43) twice. *180 sts.*
Row 37 K2, (yo, k2 tog) to end.

Row 38 Knit. Break off yarn and leave sts on a spare needle.
To make parts 3 and 4 on the diagram, work another scalloped lace edging and striped border as given above. Do not break off yarn.

CENTER PANEL

This is part 5 on the diagram. Use yarn E.
Next 2 rows Taking 1 st from sts on spare needle and next st on left-hand needle, k2 tog, k88, k2 tog and turn, k90 and turn. Rep last 2 rows until 180 rows have been worked. With right side of center panel and rem border together, bind off 90 sts taking 1 st from each needle and working them tog.

FINISHING

Join corner seams, matching stripes. Block as given on page 139, placing a pin in each of the points of the lace edging.

Techniques

Measuring your gauge

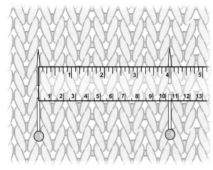

Measuring the number of stitches

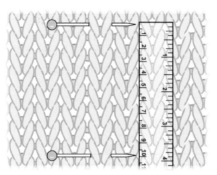

Measuring the number of rows

GAUGE

At the beginning of every pattern is a gauge measurement, such as "22 sts and 30 rows measure 4 inches (10cm) over stockinette stitch on size 6 (4mm) needles." This tells you how large the stitches are on the garment so that, by matching this gauge, you can produce a garment of the correct size. Four factors affect the gauge: needle size, stitch pattern, the yarn, and the knitter.

Needle size Larger needles produce larger stitches than smaller ones do.

Stitch pattern Different stitch patterns produce different gauges; therefore you must check your gauge each time you embark on a new project, using the stitch pattern specified.

Yarn Patterns worked in finer yarns have more stitches and rows over 4 inches (10cm) than those in thicker yarns. It is very important to check your gauge if you use a different yarn from that specified in the pattern, as even a standard weight of yarn can vary from one manufacturer to another.

The knitter Even when using the same yarn, needle size, and stitch pattern, two knitters may not produce knitting at the same gauge. If your gauge does not match that given in the pattern, you should change to a larger or smaller needle size.

Making a gauge swatch

Using the yarn, needles, and stitch pattern called for, knit a sample slightly larger than 4 inches (10cm) square. Block the sample as the finished garment would be blocked.

Being careful not to stretch it, place the swatch right side up on a flat surface and place a ruler along one row. Use pins to mark the beginning and end of a 4-inch (10cm) measurement. Count the number of stitches between the pins.

Then place the ruler vertically along one side of a column of stitches, and mark your 4-inch (10cm) measurement as before. Count the number of rows between the pins.

If you have fewer stitches and rows than stated, you should use a smaller needle; if more stitches and rows, a larger one.

If you have trouble obtaining the correct gauge with American needles, you might try the corresponding metric size (the garments were knitted on metric needles). Some of these vary slightly from the U.S. equivalent; and in one case, 3mm, there is no U.S. equivalent.

If you cannot match both the stitch and row gauge, work to the correct stitch gauge; the length can be adjusted by working more or fewer rows.

SPECIAL TECHNIQUES

Some of the patterns in this book require you to knit in the round, with circular or double-pointed needles, to knit cables, to follow color charts, or to knit with two colors of yarn in a row.

Knitting in the round

Traditional Fair Isle garments, and fisher ganseys are knitted in the round. This has

Knitting in the round

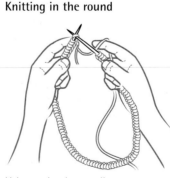

Using a circular needle

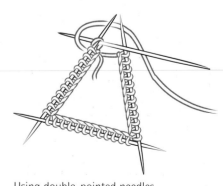

Using double-pointed needles

the advantage that there is much less sewing to do at the finishing stage. Also, the front of the work always faces you, so it is easier to follow the color or stitch pattern charts.

Circular needles are used from the beginning when knitting these garments, but a set of double-pointed needles is more useful when picking up stitches, such as for necklines or sleeves.

To mark so-called "seam" lines at every half round of a garment, use a small marker of contrasting thread. This will guide you when you have to divide for the front and back. Seamlines on ganseys are often indicated by a column of purl stitches in the pattern.

If you are using circular needles, you cast on in the usual way and knit into the first stitch to make a continuous round. You must make certain that your cast-on row is not twisted when beginning your first round. To knit stockinette stitch, simply knit every row.

If you are using a set of double-pointed needles, the stitches are divided among three of the needles (or four, if using a set of five), and the remaining one is used to knit. To close the circle, knit into the first cast-on stitch, marking this stitch with contrasting thread, and making sure no gap forms in the knitting. If you find it difficult to avoid gaps when changing from one needle to another, you can rotate this point around the work by moving two or three stitches each time you change from one needle

to another. If you do this, it is important to mark your side stitches and center back and front.

Stitch pattern charts

Simple patterns containing only knit and purl, such as those used on the fisher ganseys, can be shown on charts. In these, one symbol represents a knit stitch and one a purl stitch. When you are knitting in the round, the right side is facing, and the chart is read every row from right to left.

When the work divides at the armholes, and you are knitting backward and forward, you must read the first and all odd-numbered rows from right to left, and the second and all even-numbered rows from left to right.

Because the chart represents the right side of the work, all the wrong-side rows must be worked with the knit stitches being worked as purl, and purl stitches as knit.

Cables

A distinctive characteristic of Aran sweaters is the use of cables. These are created when stitches are moved out of position so that braided or ropelike twists are formed. This is achieved by using a special, double-pointed cable needle.

A given number of stitches are slipped onto the cable needle and held at either the front or back of the work. A number of stitches are then worked from the main needle, then the stitches on the cable needle are worked.

Stitches held at the front twist a cable from right to left when knitted off; stitches held at the back twist the cable from left to right when knitted off.

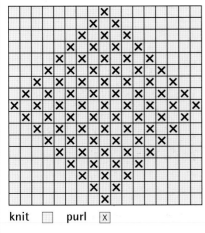

Stitch pattern chart

knit ☐ purl ☒

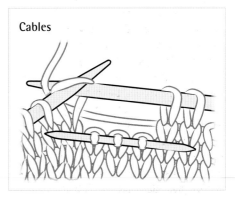

Cables

A typical colour pattern chart

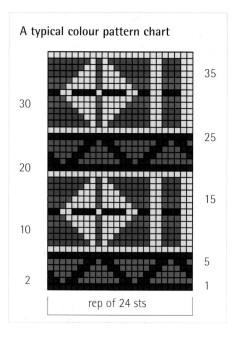

35
30
25
20
15
10
5
2
1

rep of 24 sts

Fair Isle knitting

In order to knit authentic Fair Isle, you need to knit in the round, follow a color pattern chart, and use two colors of yarn in a row.
Color pattern charts Color patterns are often given in the form of a chart, where each square represents one stitch and each line of the chart, one row. In this book the colors are indicated by colors corresponding to those used for the garment, but sometimes they are indicated by symbols. The chart is worked from bottom to top, and the rows are numbered with odd numbers on the right-hand side of the chart, and even numbers on the left. The same chart is used for circular or flat knitting, although it must be read differently.

In circular knitting, every row on the chart represents a round of knitting. Since you have the right side of the work facing you, every stitch will be a knit stitch and you read every row from right to left. Mark the beginning of each round with a stitch marker.

For flat knitting, you will knit backward and forward in stockinette stitch, so the first row (and odd-numbered rows) will be knit and the chart read from right to left. These are right-side rows. The second row (and every even-numbered row) is worked in purl and the chart read from left to right; these are wrong-side rows.

Using two colors of yarn in a row When knitting Fair Isle, the yarn that is not being used has to be carried across the back of the knitting. This is normally done by stranding; in Fair Isle there are not usually more than five stitches before a color change, so there are no long loops at the back of the fabric. The advantage of stranding, as opposed to weaving yarns into the back of the work, is that the finished fabric is softer. However, it is very important that the strands at the back of the work are not pulled too tightly—both to achieve the correct gauge (stranding too

tightly will pucker the fabric) and to produce natural give in the finished fabric. To ensure this, every time you change color, gently but firmly pull back the last ten or so stitches on the right-hand needle so that your knitting is very slightly stretched.

Joining in new yarn Try to avoid joining a new ball of yarn in the middle of a round or row. To judge whether the remaining length of yarn is long enough to complete the round or row, use this rough guideline: in stockinette stitch each round or row takes about three times the width of the knitting. In cable or texture knitting, the yarn needed is about five times the width of the knitting.

In Fair Isle, always join the new color at the beginning of a round. Break off the old yarn, leaving a few inches of spare yarn; join the new color and the finished color with a single knot, making sure the knot is close to the last stitch on your right-hand needle. Begin the next round, and weave the spare yarn into the first ten stitches of the round, then carefully trim away the excess. This weaving can be done as you knit or at the finishing stage, using a tapestry needle.

The latter method is preferable where you have several color joins over relatively few rows, and where weaving each end into the working row would create excess bulk in one place. Use the tapestry needle to run each end up or down a few rows and then darn it into the back of the work a short distance from other yarn ends.

Stranding yarn

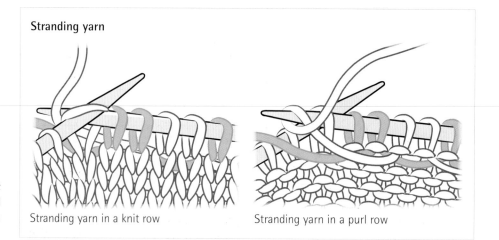

Stranding yarn in a knit row

Stranding yarn in a purl row

Sewing together—mattress stitch

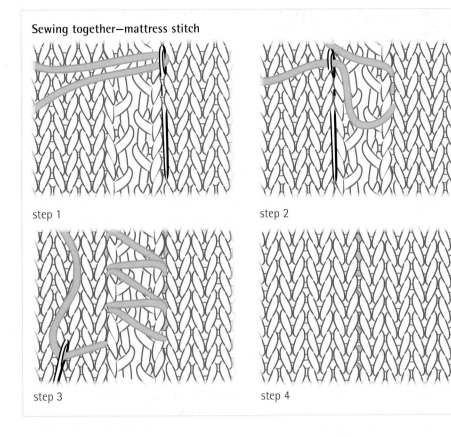

step 1

step 2

step 3

step 4

FINISHING

Blocking When you have finished knitting, the garment pieces have to be blocked and sewn together; if you have made the garment in one piece it can blocked in one piece. Pin the garment, or each garment piece, out on

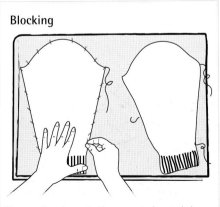

Blocking

Pin out the pieces to the correct size and shape

a flat surface to the correct measurements. The blocking surface can be a blanket or towel covered with a cotton sheet. Then spray the knitting with cold, clean water, using a spray bottle, until it is just damp; leave it to dry naturally.

The fisher ganseys are not traditionally blocked, so whether you choose to do this is up to you.

For cotton garments, pin out each piece to size and then lightly press, using a damp cloth or steam iron. Do not move the iron across the fabric, but press gently with up and down movements.

Aran garments need only light blocking, because of their heavy texture. Pin the pieces out to size, spray lightly with water, and allow to dry.

The lace wool garments are delicate but do need careful blocking in order to obtain the openwork effect. In this case, dampen the knitting lightly, and on your blocking surface very gently ease it to the correct size so that

it is slightly stretched. Where there is a pointed edge, place a pin at the bottom of each point; allow to dry naturally.

Sewing together The ideal stitch for sewing up is mattress stitch, which provides a strong, invisible seam. Place the pieces right side up with the two seam edges side by side. Using a tapestry needle, stitch through two stitch bars, one stitch in from the edge on one side. Pick up the two stitch bars one stitch in on the other side. Without pulling the yarn taut, pick up the next two stitch bars on the first side. Then pick up the next two stitch bars on the other side, and so on.

When the yarn is looped from one edge to the other about five times, pull it taut to draw the seam together. Continue until the seam is complete.

For joining curved edges, as for a set-in sleeve, backstitch, as used in dressmaking, is most useful. Slipstitch is used for hemming neckbands in place and catching down pocket linings, for example.

Washing

After spending a lot of time and trouble hand-knitting a sweater, it pays to wash it with care. A lot of yarns now may be safely machine washed, so always check the yarn label for care instructions, and keep a label for reference.

Shetland yarns, however, must be washed by hand. Using a wool detergent, and hand-warm water, gently immerse the garment and squeeze it in the suds for a few minutes. Do not rub or soak it. Rinse in the same temperature several times to remove all the detergent and until the water is clear.

Place the garment in a thick towel and roll it up. Press the roll with your hands to remove as much water as possible. Alternatively, put the garment in a pillowcase and give it a very short, fast spin in a washing machine. Then spread it on a clean towel on a rack over the bathtub to dry naturally.

Guernsey-wool garments should be washed and dried in the same way.

Never hang knitted garments on a hanger, but always store them folded flat in a drawer or on a shelf.

Directory of Sweaters

Below is a directory of all the garments featured in this book, from chunky ganseys for cold days by the sea to delicate Shetland lace coverups. The soft, earthy palette used throughout has been inspired by the natural colors of the countryside.

Flamborough Fisherman's Gansey p30

Polperro Pattern Jacket p33

Newbiggin Pattern Sweater p36

Short-Sleeve Cotton Shirt p38

Jacob's Ladder Sweater p40

Fife Banded Gansey p42

Sanquhar Gansey p45

Eriskay Gansey p47

Caister Fisherman's Gansey p54

Cross and Flower Fair Isle Crewneck p70

Cross and Square Fair Isle Vest p72

Diamond Fair Isle Vest p74

Katie's Fair Isle Vest p76

OXO Fair Isle Crewneck p78

Cable and Moss Aran Tunic p96

Chevron Aran Crewneck p98

Tree of Life Aran Jacket p101

Wheat Cable Cotton Sweater p105

Fountain Lace Short-Sleeve Sweater p108

Classic Cotton Crewneck p110

New Shell Pattern Lace Sweater p126

Lace Cardigan in Eyelet Pattern p128

Old Shell Pattern Lace Sweater p130

Fern Motif Sweater p132

Old Shell Shetland Shawl p134

Resources

FRANGIPANI

Caunce Head
Predannack
Mullion
Cornwall TR12 7HA
UK
+ 44 (0) 1326 240128
www.guernseywool.co.uk

IRISS OF PENZANCE

66 Chapel Street
Penzance
Cornwall TR18 4AD
UK
+ 44 (0) 1736 36656
www.iriss.co.uk/ganseys
sales@iriss.co.uk
For Wendy (Poppleton's) 5-ply Guernsey wool

JAMIESON & SMITH
(SHETLAND WOOL BROKERS) LTD

90 North Road
Lerwick
Shetland Isles ZE1 0PQ
UK
+ 44 (0) 1595 693579
www.shetland-wool-brokers.zetnet.co.uk
sales@shetlandwoolbrokers.co.uk

JAMIESON'S SPINNING (SHETLAND) LTD

Sandness
Shetland Isles ZE2 99
UK
+ 44 (0) 1595 693114
www.jamiesonsofshetland.co.uk
info@jamiesonsofshetland.co.uk

SCHOOLHOUSE PRESS

6899 Cary Bluff
Pittsville, WI 54466
USA
800.850.5648
www.schoolhousepress.com
info@schoolhousepress.com
For Jamieson & Smith Shetland yarns,
and Poppleton's Guernsey wool

SIMPLY SHETLAND

18435 Olympic Avenue South
Seattle, WA 98188
USA
001.253.859.1800
www.simplyshetland.net
info@simplyshetland.net
For Jamieson's Shetland yarn

THE YARN BARN

5077 Andersonville Road
Dilllwyn, VA 23936
USA
800.850.6008
www.yarnbarn.com
info@yarnbarn.com
For Frangipani 5-ply Guernsey wool

WESTMINSTER FIBERS INC.

165 Ledge Street
Nashua, NH 03060
USA
1.800.445.9272
www.westminsterfibers.com
For your nearest outlet for Rowan yarns

Acknowledgments

First of all, I would like to thank Jacqui Small, who chose this book to add to her craft list, and her team, who have brought this project to fruition.

Many thanks particularly to Margaret Stuart, in Shetland, who managed to find knitters still able and willing to knit up the Fair Isle and lace garments—they are now few and far between. Thanks to all the other knitters who undertook the projects against deadlines, who already have busy lives; and to Pauline Hornsby, who checked patterns when needed and helped to smooth out any little technical problems. It has been a pleasure working with everyone who has contributed to the finished book—it has rekindled many happy memories.

Madeline Weston

Knitters

Ganseys
Sarah Crowther
Abi Flynn-Jones
Jackie Hall
Pauline Hornsby
Helen Llamas
Margaret MacInnes
Lou Sugg

Fair Isle
Grace Anderson
Pearl Johnson
Barbara Reid
Katie Simpson
Julia Smith

Aran
Joyce Coombs
Sarah Crowther
Pauline Hornsby
Claire Hurley
Susan Smith

Shetland lace
Margaret Doull
Ina Irvine
Wilma Couper